UFOs Are with Us—Take My Word

UFOs Are with Us—
Take My Word

by

Leo Dworshak

DORRANCE PUBLISHING CO., INC.
PITTSBURGH, PENNSYLVANIA 15222

ISBN # 0-8059-5868-1

Printed in the United States of America

First Printing
For information or to order additional books, please write:
Dorrance Publishing Co., Inc.
643 Smithfield Street
Pittsburgh, Pennsylvania 15222
U.S.A.
1-800-788-7654
Or visit our web site and on-line catalog at
www.dorrancepublishing.com

Dedication

In memory of my brother, Michael Dworshak,
who died in Korea in 1950.

Preface

AFTER CONSIDERING the comments of the many kind people who have read this account while I was preparing it for publication. I understood that it was important to clarify a few points for the reader.

First of all, I am not a professional writer. Before my retirement, I made my living in the construction industry, where I stand on my reputation for honesty and customer satisfaction. The account I have written is not a science fiction novel where the author has all the answers. To this day, I can only guess at the reasons and meanings behind many of my experiences and memories—I do not have all the answers.

I wrote the first draft of this account in the early 1950s, after we were notified that my brother Mike had been killed in combat in Korea. I realized that with him gone, there was no other living person who had seen and experienced these events. I knew that it was up to me to leave a record of what happened, why I believe the things I do today, and what is important for us, humanity, to strive for in the future.

What Mike and I did in 1932 was not heroic, it was more a matter of determination. It was Mike's determination that carried us through a lot of disappointment to the most important events of our lives. He was also the only other person who shared the frustration of never being believed. This was a very big thing for both of us to deal with in our lives. Military service carried us both away from the places and times in this account. When we returned to our home, the world was somehow different from what we remembered of our childhood. Times were still very tough at home and the war had not helped us much.

Much of my understanding about the significance of one or another part of our experience developed only later in my life, after I was able to put together my experiences with the developments in science and engineering we have seen in recent years.

Unexplainable Experience

One late afternoon in the summer of the year 1932, when I was a twelve-year-old North Dakota farm boy, my brother Mike and I experienced the first of an extraordinary series of events that changed my life forever. It is something that is very hard for me to explain so that you will understand as you read this story. I will never be able to meet most of my readers, but I hope many of you are young people, because I was a youngster when most of these things happened to me. I think young readers will know why Mike and I did many of the things we did back then, why we asked some questions and did not ask others. As you will see if you read further, many strange and unusual experiences happened to us back then and have continued into my later life. I believe that it is important to explain to you just what happened to us then, because the years have shown me the truth of what I learned. I have tried my best to remember everything that happened to me and accurately describe what I heard and saw and how I felt.

As I said, I was a farm kid. My parents immigrated to the United States from Germany. My father, among his many other business activities, was a farmer and much like what we today might call a "custom combiner." He owned and operated a steam thrashing rig throughout North Dakota and into Canada. When Dad was operating the thrashing machine near home, I got to go along with the work crew when I was still very young. They started at six in the morning and worked through until six in the evening. My job was to blow the whistle on the steam engine for lunch breaks at ten o'clock and twelve-thirty and finally at six when it was time to quit.

Harvest back then was quite different from today. The stalks of grain were cut, raked up, loaded on wagons and hauled to a central point, and stacked in piles five feet apart. The crew would then pull the thrashing machine between the stacks and two men on each stack would use pitchforks to throw the stalks into the thrashing machine, which would separate the grain from the straw and chaff. Working with the thrashing crew was very exciting for me, but when they moved too far away, I had to stay home with Mom and my little brothers. Since I was the oldest, most of the chores were my responsibility, and there was always plenty to do.

I guess we lived on a pretty average farm for those times and that part of the country. We had a barn and all kinds of outbuildings: chicken coops, an ice house, a livestock shelter, pens, and a well. I hauled water and coal and wood fuel for the stove. I fed chickens, geese, pigs, and horses and milked the cow, just like every other farm kid, every day. But there was still plenty of time to go hunting and exploring across the foothills of the Killdeer Mountains around our farm. I had a shotgun and often brought back prairie chickens and pinfeather ducks for Mom to cook. Chinese pheasants had been introduced some years before and were spreading throughout the farmlands, but the prairie chickens were still our favorites. Many times when we wandered in the hills around our place, we weren't really hunting, just exploring, looking for some kind of excitement. There wasn't much variation in our life. It always seemed to be just work, work, work.

Every day, after we finished the morning chores and filled our bellies with Mom's tasty lunch, we took off exploring, fishing, and hunting in the hills and fields. There were other kids around, but we kept mostly to ourselves. We rambled around poking into badger holes, looking for skunks, and trying to get the drop on the prairie chickens while swarms of grasshoppers crackled and buzzed around us. It seemed like the hoppers were thicker that year than ever before. Each year they just seemed to get worse. We heard that the government had been spraying a new chemical called DDT in other states to kill the grasshoppers and mosquitoes, but we just had to suffer with them. Nothing seemed to help. Sometimes the hoppers just picked a field, started in at the edge, and ate it all up, right in to the center. We could tell Mom and Dad were worried about the crops. Between the hoppers and the drought, there were not many crops left. When the crops were poor, Dad's thrashing business suffered, so he started working a gravel pit to help make ends meet.

It all began on that one ordinary summer day, about one-and-a-half miles east of Killdeer, North Dakota, the nearest and only town around. Dad was off somewhere with the thrashing crew, so we had to keep ourselves occupied that afternoon. My younger brother Mike and I climbed up to a grassy hilltop in the hot summer sun. Mike immediately spotted a strange object down in the valley just below us.

"Leo, look," he whispered in German, as we all spoke German in our house. He was pointing his finger like he would point out a pheasant or a jack rabbit.

It was a huge, round thing, as big as our barn at least. We just stood there gaping at it and began excitedly discussing what it was doing down there and trying our best to understand just what we were seeing. We were no strangers to machinery, from steam engines to trucks and farm equipment of every description. We had seen the railroad locomotives and even lived with the luxury of a Model T Ford, which Dad bought for $397. This building or machine was completely unlike anything we had ever seen or heard of before. It was silvery, and although it was probably more than half a mile away, we could tell it was certainly as big as our barn, maybe even bigger. It appeared to be perfectly round, not round like a baseball, unless you could kind of flatten a baseball a little bit and put kind of a bump or blister on the top, but round more like a silver dollar. I counted many different colors of light on it that came from a band around the edge.

I thought it must be a machine because it was rotating in a complicated way. The flashing colored lights formed an outer shell, like a band or belt that went completely around it at the widest point and was turning one way. The inner shell seemed to be standing still or perhaps turning the other way. The colored lights came only from the rotating shell or belt. Unlike every other large machine we had ever seen in operation, it was totally silent and produced no cloud of exhaust fumes or smoke. It surely wasn't a steam engine.

We stood there on the hilltop for some time, just watching that incredible machine flashing its lights and rotating in its strange and amazing way. Then we decided to try to get closer for a better look. As we began to walk downhill toward the machine, we were still more amazed to find our way blocked by an invisible force that would not let us get any closer. It was as if we were bumping up against an invisible fence or wall.

We encountered that invisible "something" again and again, sliding to one side and the other against its unyielding surface. Finally we gave up our efforts to approach it and just sat on the hillside next to the barrier, watching the machine and debating the situation. Mike was pretty young, but he was always smart and full of questions. I had plenty of my own. How was it possible that an invisible "something" could block our way? How had this huge machine come to be in this valley? There was no road here. There were no tracks to it. How could something so huge appear in our valley? Why did it have all those lights? How could one part rotate and the other part stay still? How could it be so completely silent? You would come away from the thrashing machine almost deaf, and you could hear it and the steam tractor engine for miles when it was in operation. This was unlike any machine Dad or the elevator man or anybody else had ever talked about. We knew all about the huge steel battleships that had fought in the War. (We didn't call it

"World War I." We just called it "the War," with a small *t* and a capital *W*). But the huge ships we imagined floated on the ocean. Here, the nearest water was Killdeer Creek, and then only early in the spring. The creek was almost completely dried up now, except for a few isolated bogs, our deep swimming hole spots and some mud holes. Even during high water, we decided, the creek couldn't float this thing.

If we had seen such a sight twenty years later, I am sure our reactions and speculations would have been much different. We would have evaluated what we saw by adult standards and made adult speculations about its meaning and purpose. As it was, we were very curious about an interesting new object in our world.

We tried to approach it over and over again. We even went back over the top of the hill, around the side, and came up on it from a different direction, but found we could not get closer by any route. Finally we just sat back down and watched. Before too long, we saw the curious rotation slow and eventually stop, and the colorful lights stopped blinking at the edge of the machine. We also noticed that the outer shell now had an opening. I called it a door, but it was nothing at all like a barn door or a house door that hinged out and away from the building. It had somehow opened up in the side of the machine. This unusual door just opened up. Out of it came three people who walked down a sort of ramp that, just as miraculously, sprouted out of the side of the machine. They stood in the dry weeds beside their enormous, silvery machine. It had to be a mechanical thing because it looked so much like polished metal. How could they just open the door through a wall when, moments before, there was no sign of a door? How could that ramp appear and grow silently out of the side of the machine? We had seen no one carry it into place.

We watched the distant figures very closely and saw that they were all wearing the same type and color of suit or coverall. These people walked only a short distance away from the machine and moved around near it. They would look up at the sky, as if they were thankful and pleased with the weather. We excitedly talked to each other about why they had brought the machine to this remote valley. We had hiked through this valley before and there was no sign of any machine. It was no different from dozens of similar spots we had explored, just a hot and dusty depression in the hills with lots of grasshoppers buzzing around. Only later would we begin to understand the reason for their intense interest in the sky and our planet Earth.

There was no other movement down in the valley except these people walking around. We watched them closely, but they were too far away for us to see much detail. They finally returned to the machine and closed the door, and the ramp just went away again. We were sorry we didn't have a chance to clearly see how they looked or hear how they talked. I timed our stay there by the height of the sun in the sky and knew we had to make it home in time for dinner. I wanted to stay, but I knew we had to leave. We decided and planned at that moment to return at the first opportunity tomorrow to see if the men would come out of the machine again. It was a mile and a half walk from our house, but we wanted very much to study these people and their huge, silvery, spinning light machine more closely. This was the most exciting thing we had ever seen. We wanted to stay longer and watch the machine in case they came out again, but we finally had to leave on the run for home. We knew Mom would be worried and angry if we were late for dinner and maybe wouldn't let us come back out again tomorrow.

As we trudged back home, our mood alternated from excited talking to silent thoughts about what we had seen. I think it is important that we never thought, then or later on, of the people we had seen as being anything but men, people like ourselves.

The following day, Mike and I wrapped cold pancakes smeared with butter and sprinkled with sugar in a handkerchief for our lunch and left about midmorning. We hiked directly back to the very same spot where we first saw the huge, round, lighted machine. You can just imagine our total amazement when it was nowhere to be seen! We knew we had the right hill and the right valley, but that huge thing was gone. We backtracked along yesterday's trail and confirmed our location again. There wasn't the slightest doubt about it. This was the right valley, but there was no machine. How could it be? How could they move that huge machine?

There was nothing else for us to do but turn around and leave. Mike was close to tears and I wasn't much better off. We were so sure it would be there and so terribly disappointed when we couldn't find it again. Were we just "seeing things"? As we walked back home, we argued back and forth about what was happening in that valley and our mood began to change. We began to get excited again about the many new questions this latest experience raised concerning that puzzling machine. It clearly had even more wonderful properties than we had imagined. We began to wonder about ourselves. Were we going loony? How could such a huge thing be there one day and gone the next? Were we seeing things because we were sick?

Everyone feared getting sick, because the doctor had to be paid—somehow. We knew folks who didn't have any money and had to beg the doctor to take a chicken for payment. I even felt Mike's head and he felt mine. I didn't feel sick. We knew what we had seen. Why was this complicated machine here in the Killdeer Mountains in North Dakota on one day and gone the next? Where had the men gone? What had they done with the machine? We thought of the process of moving the thrashing equipment and hauling the wagons and trucks full of grain. That machine was bigger than our own barn. It must weigh a tremendous amount. How could those three men move it without leaving a trail? Our minds were buzzing and our curiosity was eating us alive.

Three days later, we hiked back to the spot again and found no sign of the machine. We somehow knew the men were nowhere about either. We searched the valley and the nearby hills on the off chance that we had somehow returned to the wrong valley, but they had just plain disappeared.

Several hot, dusty trips through the area came after that, with no greater success. It was two weeks before Mike and I saw them again. It was midafternoon as we stood in the same valley, looking at the ground, and puzzling about how there was no sign that anyone had even walked here. I cannot explain why, but our senses somehow told us to look up. There, high in the sky and almost straight above us, we saw the machine. It was flying! It was an airship! Some of our questions were answered, but many new questions began to appear in their place. We quickly moved back up the hillside and out of the way behind some bushes. The airship we had spotted in the sky was slowly nearing the valley floor. It was clearly coming in for a landing. We could sense a strange stillness that grew about us. This stillness gave us the first hint I can remember of a feeling that these people could stop all movement around them at any given time. Was it the same force that could propel this strange vessel through the air without a sound?

I am certain we were the only witnesses to the ship's landing. It felt very strange to us to see this huge ship landing in the very spot where we had stood just a few minutes before. The appearance of the ship was the same as we remembered from our first sighting—a mirror-like exterior with a central rotating band that emitted colored lights. When the ship came to rest, the rotating band slowed to a stop, and the lights went out as before.

Trying to approach the ship again, we were blocked once more by that strange "something" that was transparent, both there and not there. Although we could see right through it, we were still blocked from moving any closer. Looking about us, we noticed nothing was moving, not a blade of grass or the branches on the bushes.

While we sat by the barrier and watched this huge machine, the strange door started to open again. A total of six men emerged from the door and walked down the ramp. They were dressed in a different kind of uniform than when we first saw them, but we were somehow certain they were the same men as we saw before. We were close enough to see that they now wore a shirt-slack type of clothing that looked quite comfortable. We wished we had such fine clothes, instead of our ragged overalls and patched cotton shirts.

The men began doing something that looked peculiar to us. We couldn't figure out what they were up to. All six men would repeatedly reach down to the ground and apparently pick up something from the earth. Whether or not they took it with them, we could not tell. I don't know why, but I was convinced they could see us and knew we were there. We could clearly see them moving about, unconcerned about our presence. After Mike and I watched for an hour or more, I turned to him and said, "It's about time we were heading for home." Our farm was directly west of this area, not far out of Killdeer. He and I were not happy about leaving, but the length of the shadows and the position of the sun told us our time that day was up. We reluctantly turned our backs on the men and their airship and began walking for home.

During our walk home that evening, Mike and I decided to tell our parents about what we had just seen and get their opinion about our experience. That night at dinner, Mom and Dad listened patiently to our excited story. They agreed with us that something like this machine, this airship, could exist, but advised us just to forget about everything we had told them. We couldn't believe it! They didn't seem to want to talk about it and definitely didn't share our excitement. We were very, very disappointed at their response to what was for us the most exciting experience of our lives.

After the dinner dishes were done, Mike went outside, and I went up to my room. I lay in bed with dozens of thoughts of the strange airship and its passengers running through my mind. I just couldn't forget about what we had seen. It kept going through my mind over and over. I guess it was there to stay, whether Mom or Dad or anybody liked it or not.

The next day, after morning chores and breakfast were over, I found Mike out in the back yard. "How would you like to walk into town with me?" I asked.

"Sure, nothing else to do," he replied. "Might just as well." Our parents' response to our tale of the airship was on his mind too.

"I wanted to talk to Mr. Brooks down at the elevator," I told him, "and see what he makes of this." Mr. Brooks was our local "man of the world" who had seen more than most of us local folks. He would know if the amazing ship with its invisible wall and neatly uniformed passengers was written up in the many magazines and newspapers that he kept in the office.

Mr. Brooks was about the only older man in town who would take us kids seriously no matter what we told him; if it was important to us he would talk to us about it. He was an average man with graying hair and dusty old overalls, who seemed to have all the answers or a good story to tell.

"He'll know if they're spraying the hoppers," Mike allowed. One of our theories about the machine was that it was a new government plan for killing the hoards of grasshoppers that were eating our crops. We thought these people might be part of a government project to spray the countryside with DDT, a new chemical that was supposed to kill troublesome insects like grasshoppers and mosquitoes.

Arriving at the elevator, we found Mr. Brooks studying his ledger books in his dusty little office and I told him about our experiences. Since I was the oldest, Mike kind of hung back and let me do the talking. I told Mr. Brooks we had seen some kind of airship, and thought he might think we were a little bit squirrelly, but wanted to ask him about it anyway.

He looked at us and said, "Boys, I don't think you are crazy, because I experienced the same thing when I was out on the side roads one evening. It was on an evening just like this. I saw one of those things flying through the air without a sound. It was definitely some kind of airship, and boys, I feel just tremendous that you have seen this ship too. What I saw fits right in with what you have seen. I always felt like I wanted to tell someone, but I knew no one would believe me, so I just kept my mouth shut. Business is bad enough as it is."

Mr. Brooks then talked at length about airplanes and zeppelins, and explained how they did many fantastic and terrible things in the War. "One thing, boys," he said, "they all make noise. What we saw don't make any noise at all." It was true. The airplanes all had powerful engines that could be heard for miles around. The zeppelins were hard for us to imagine, but we knew they were tremendous machines with many powerful and noisy engines.

"You'd be able to hear a zeppelin coming," Mike affirmed.

Mr. Brooks talked a great deal about the War, and then went on to his outrage at the government's latest foolishness, our ship forgotten.

"They're buying up all the cattle at five dollars a head, boys, shooting 'em, and burying 'em in a trench to rot. Our bellies are crying for beefsteak, and the government puts it in the ground to rot! That don't make any sense at all, does it, boys?" By that time, it was starting to get quite dark and we had to leave for home.

On the way home from town, we debated our situation further and decided that somehow or other, no matter what, we must meet the people from that ship. We didn't foresee the difficulty we would experience in this undertaking. Mr. Brooks' comments had planted the seed, and by the time we returned home, we had come to the conclusion that this machine had to be a spaceship, because it came silently from the sky. Our sightings matched and expanded upon what Mr. Brooks had seen. He was our authority on the world beyond Killdeer. He said men had never produced anything like it before, so we reasoned it had to be a spaceship from somewhere beyond. We didn't tell Mr. Brooks about the invisible wall. He was too upset about the cattle and the weather and all the farm auctions to listen.

In those days, people did not even mention things like what we had seen. No one we knew ever mentioned anything like spaceships. The talk was about the drought and the depression and the government and local doings like who was driving an automobile and who was drunk on moonshine and fighting out by the stockyards. There were many bloody tales about the doings of big-city gangsters and bank robbers. When we heard that a large sum of cash had been stolen in a distant city, each of us secretly dreamed what we could do with that money. Many families went broke in those times and gave up, auctioning the farm to pay the bills and then leaving town. That is part of the reason Mike and I were not afraid when we first saw the ship and the men. I felt that they would do us no harm and might, in some way, help us out. I don't know why I felt like that, but I was convinced we were safe with them. We didn't have anything to lose. Maybe our experiences with these strangers in their fantastic ship would lead us to something better than our farm and the dusty streets of Killdeer.

Things were tough on everybody in those depression days. Hunting, fishing, and trapping was a way of life for everyone, but particularly for us kids. We could earn twenty-five or thirty cents by selling a muskrat skin and have enough to attend a moving picture show. In those days, a show ticket was only five cents, but we never seemed to have the five cents to spare. Government relief and work programs were a big part of our lives. There was a county nurse who came out to the house once a month to check on everything and give us a lecture. Families could qualify for relief food and men could join the WPA to earn forty dollars a month for forty hours of hard work each week.

We were unable to forget that the fantastic machine did actually exist, and were determined to investigate it further. We took every opportunity to walk back to the valley to see if the ship had returned. Each time that we returned to the spot where the spaceship had landed, we looked around the area and tried to figure out why it would land on this opening, which lay in a very ordinary little valley with hills all around it. Why was this place so interesting to them that they returned over and over again? The area was about one mile across and maybe a half-mile wide.

While we were studying the area early one afternoon, our persistence was rewarded and we again watched the ship come in for a landing. This time, we were about eight hundred feet from the spaceship when we encountered their invisible wall, the closest we had been to them yet. I still figured there must be some way we could get closer, and somehow get to talk to these men. We waved and hollered, but to no avail. We were unable to draw their attention.

We knew that if this spaceship would just keep coming back, maybe there would be a chance that we could get closer and draw their attention. Just maybe, we might have a chance to get acquainted with them. Soon, we saw the sun was again settling low and decided that we were not going to make any more headway that day.

"Mike, maybe we had just better be heading for home," I said. "No sense in sticking around here."

"Leo, maybe the sun is in their eyes and they can't see us. Maybe we can—"

"They can see us, all right. They're just ignoring us because they don't want to scare us." There was no reason I should think that. Where did I come up with that idea?

As usual, Mike didn't want to leave, but he couldn't argue that we'd be in trouble if we were late for dinner. We reluctantly turned our back on the ship and trudged over the dusty hilltop toward home, the buzzing grasshoppers often smacking us in the face as we walked. As the hot dry summer progressed, the earth cracked open from the heat. Swarms of grasshoppers would start at the edges of the farmers' fields and eat them bare to the center. Sometimes the hoppers would gnaw at the stalk of the wheat plants, right below the developing head of grain, but only enough to cause the head to wither and fall off. It was like they intended to spoil what they could not eat. The farmers would cut the ruined fields early for hay, since there was no hay to feed the cattle on the ranches. A plant called Russian Thistle had invaded the fields and barren ground everywhere. The dead thistle plants broke loose and blew across the open country like big balls that were sometimes a couple of feet across. Some people called them tumbleweeds. The desperate and ever-thrifty ranchers were even cutting the young thistle plants as feed for their hungry cattle.

Anytime we mentioned our fantastic experiences to our parents or to some other people we knew, we were always advised just to forget about this ship. It would be better for all concerned, they said. Just listening to them made us more determined than ever to figure out what was going on. We decided never to give up.

Early the next morning, Mike and I hiked back to the area. Our trail to the valley went across some ground that belonged to some people by the name of Flecks. It was quite a hike across those hills, and when we arrived on the spot, the ship was not there. As we moved closer to the spot where the ship should have been, my brother said "Are you sure we are not just going crazy?"

"No, Mike, I don't think so. Why don't we hike down to where that ship was sitting? Maybe we can find something to prove that we aren't just imagining all this."

It was like that. We would work up our enthusiasm and our belief when we saw the ship, but the enthusiasm would die down after trips when we found nothing. On one trip I would be enthusiastic and hopeful, but Mike would be doubting our sanity. The next time he would be up and I would be down. We hadn't touched the ship. We hadn't spoken to the men. We couldn't even get closer to them than the hilltop perch when they were there. We searched the surface of the ground very closely but found no markings of any kind where that tremendous machine had landed and the men had been walking only the night before. None of the weeds were mashed down. There were no footprints but our own. The earth was completely undisturbed. Not a single dry blade of grass had been disturbed. There was nothing to be found—nothing at all. I thought it was mighty strange that there was no sign of any heavy object having landed there. It never occurred to me that, although it was quite large, the ship might not be very heavy at all. I thought surely those four mighty prongs beneath the ship would have left some holes in the ground.

We made many more futile trips to the place where we had first seen the spaceship land. Sometimes I couldn't think of anything else but that huge machine. After what we had experienced, no other kid could possibly feel any different. It was the biggest thing in our lives. My mom often wondered what we were doing out there all the time, but my father always seemed to be off someplace working. When there was no work for the thrashing machine, he used his trucks and equipment in the gravel pit and often didn't return home until late in the evenings.

One afternoon we returned to the valley, found the ship in the same location, and settled into our usual spot below the top of a hill. We picked the spot because it gave us a good view of anything happening down there and was out of the sun.

Mike and I found, as usual, that it was impossible to get closer to the spaceship. A jackrabbit came running up toward us. As he passed, he ran into the same wall that confronted us. The surprised jackrabbit had been going at a pretty good clip when he hit the wall, but simply bounced off and seemed unhurt. The rabbit nuzzled up against the wall with what must have been a sore nose, moved along it one way and the other, and then just hopped off. Our senses told us these were friendly people who came to our part of the country as interested visitors, and not to be afraid, because they would not harm us any more than that jackrabbit. But there was more to it than that. We got a peaceful feeling from them. Their movements near the ship were peaceful and purposeful. I got the feeling they probably were making a survey of some kind.

As always, when we found ourselves unable to get any closer to the ship, we fell to discussing our situation and speculating about the men and their purposes. We always thought of them as men, people, humans like us. After talking about it for what seemed to be several hours, we became more convinced that they must be from some other world—somewhere besides Earth. How could a couple of farm kids think up things like that? How could we imagine a place that was not only away from us, like Paris, but a tremendous distance away from our very own world? But again, in our minds, we felt this could not be. They simply could not fly that far or that fast.

"No one," my brother said, "could fly that far. I can't believe it." Neither of us could quite accept the fact that these people might be from a very distant planet, yet both of us were able to sit there and think about the possibility. We weren't college professors or politicians or military commanders, just a couple of little kids. If we could think about these things and not get scared, why couldn't adults do the same? Where could we possibly be getting such ideas?

Abruptly, the ground began vibrating. There was no sound, but we could distinctly feel the earth vibrating. This vibration continued for long moments until we wondered what was going to happen. Then we heard a slight hum, and the vibration ended. It was the first time I ever heard anything like a mechanical sound associated with the ship. The outer shell of the ship started turning, rotating faster and faster with perfect smoothness.

Then it suddenly started rising. Those four tremendous prongs, which were maybe four feet by eight feet, began receding into the body of this flying machine. Again the earth started vibrating and we heard this slight hum. It was not loud enough to draw attention for any distance at all. Then the ship started lifting higher, going straight up. A tremendous amount of colored light flashed out from the ship. It kept going straight up. The speed was so great that when it got about ten or fifteen feet off the ground, it completely vanished. To us, it seemed like the takeoff happened in a very few seconds. We watched the ship disappear before our eyes. It was unbelievable to us then that the ship was so fast we could not keep track of it. Other than that faint hum, there was no sound made by the ship.

"I sure wish we had a camera," my brother said. "Should have got a picture. Maybe people would believe us then." The thought of us owning a camera, buying films and paying to have the photographs printed was absurd, but it was pleasant to pretend. We had seen photographs when we traveled to visit relatives, and even had some at home.

"They wouldn't let us close enough to them to take a picture," I replied. "They probably wouldn't let us take a picture, anyhow, even if we were close enough."

My brother's voice reflected some frustration as he replied, "They are not going to hurt us. We have to prove it flies around here. It must land in other spots too."

We tried to see which direction they were traveling, but they were gone before we knew it. It was impossible to see which direction they went.

On our return home, we concluded that the ship must travel in some type of cycle. A belief was growing in us that the ship followed a regular pattern. We knew they would return to this same spot again when their schedule called for another visit.

On our arrival back home, my thoughts returned to the ordinary things we were doing before we discovered that ship. Chores about the place always had to be done before Dad got back. It was best to dismiss my thoughts about that ship for the time being and get to work.

Alone in my room that night, my thoughts drifted back to the scene of the ship taking off. I became more determined for Mike and me to see more of that ship. Strange thoughts and ideas struggled with the ordinary impressions of my life. Ducks and cows and water buckets mingled with stars and planets and speeds too fast to register on the human eye. To me, there was nothing at all unusual about it. I was not aware of the many changes that were taking place in my thinking and understanding because I was on the inside looking out. I didn't know it then, but at least one other member of the family was beginning to sense the changes that were taking place within our minds.

Whenever the chores were caught up and there was not much left to be done about the place, Mike and I returned to the spaceship valley. We sat on our hillside spot where we could watch the ship. That is, if it showed up that day.

"The heck with it," Mike said. "It just isn't going to be here. It was just a darn long trip across Mr. Fleck's place, up and down those darn hills for nothing. I am getting mighty tired of it."

Again, I tried to convince Mike that we should make another trip if we couldn't accomplish this time what we had set out to do. Now we would have to leave. No sense sticking around. They probably would not show up at all today. It was just another day wasted.

"Mike, before we leave, let's go down again," I said. "Maybe this time we can come up with something. There is no harm trying."

Down the side of the hill we went, slipping and sliding, until we reached the bottom. As we started to walk over to the place where the ship had landed, a weird feeling came over me, passing as quickly as it came. It was that kind of feeling you get when someone is watching you, but you can't see them. We found nothing—no discharge or marks of any kind.

Leaving the area where the ship had landed, Mike and I climbed again to the top of the hill and headed back home.

"Well, I guess that is that. I wonder if they will ever come back?" Mike asked.

"I bet they come back, Mike," I said. "We just have to be ready for them. How we do that I don't know, but we'll think of something."

Mom was in the kitchen when we reached home. We dropped into chairs at the table, hoping for a snack before supper. She had been listening to us arguing about the ship out in the yard before we came into the house.

"Are you kids losing your senses?" she asked with a heavy sigh. "You must realize that you both have big imaginations. You should not talk about strange things like this all the time. All this going on about 'spaceships' and 'planets' and 'lights' is useless talk. Who is telling you about all these things? Is it that Mr. Brooks at the elevator?"

We told her again how we felt—that we were not imagining this, and we asked her to go along with us.

"Boys, I am not going to hike that far with you," she replied. "You will have to go without me. I've got too much to do around the house to keep you and your father and your little brother fed and in clean clothes and a clean house. I have to take care of myself so the new baby will be healthy." Mike and I both new that Mom was pregnant and had to be careful not to fall or lift anything too heavy. We tried to do as much as we could to help her because she always seemed to be tired. She must have seen the dejected looks on our faces.

"If this is what you feel you've got to do, I guess that is what it will have to be. Just don't come home with those imaginary stories, because I feel that is all they are."

Although Mom was not very encouraging, we learned not to approach Dad on the subject at all. One time, when we told him what we had seen, his reply to us was, "Boys, this is going too far. It is getting worse. You are just going to have to forget about it. I guess I'm going to have to find more work around the place to keep you busy enough so you won't have time to think about this kind of foolishness. I know something to help keep you out of trouble."

Well, I guess that took care of that. The next thing you know, he had us out cleaning the chicken house and fixing the fence.

We said nothing to Dad and took off early the following evening. Again we found nothing, which added greatly to our disappointment. Were we both having illusions, or was the experience actually real? Maybe Mom and Dad were right after all.

"That machine does exist, Leo," Mike said. "We both saw it with our own eyes. We know that it was here. No one can ever take that away from us—never!"

"Well, boys," Mother said when we returned. "Did you find anything? Did you see it, or was it all just in your head? Do you actually think you saw a spaceship?"

I hung my head, "No, we didn't see it."

"Now listen, boys," Mother said. "All you are doing is going out there and dreaming about it. You are imagining all this. You think about it and talk about it so much that you are actually beginning to think you have seen this spaceship. You are imagining all of it."

With those words ringing in my ears, I went outside with Mike. We decided to go into town and have another talk with Mr. Brooks. He always seemed to have confidence in us when we talked with him before. How could Mom see anything wrong with telling us stories about the great zeppelins, airplanes, and steel ships that floated on the water?

Mike and I hiked into town and headed straight for the elevator. Mr.

Brooks operated the only elevator in town. When we got to the elevator, we found him sitting in his chair, smoking his pipe. "Well," he said. "What can I do for you two today?"

"Mr. Brooks," I replied, "we really have seen a spaceship."

"We saw it again last week," Mike added.

"Boys," he said, "I know you are not just seeing things because I have known you boys for a long time, and I can believe you. When you tell me what you saw, I have no doubts about it. You will have to understand that only you know what you have seen and experienced. If no one else believes you, you will just have to live with it. I know—I have seen it too. I don't believe you kids are crazy. I really believe you have seen this machine. The only difference between my experience and yours is that you saw it sitting on the ground, and I saw it flying. It was the most beautiful thing I have ever seen," he said wistfully as he puffed on his pipe.

After leaving Mr. Brooks, Mike and I decided we would tell other people in town about our experience and see if we could bring another person to our valley to witness the ship and its passengers. We wandered around town until we found our friend Jeff and some other kids we knew. They were trying to find a piece of rope long enough to hang a worn-out tire in one of the big cottonwood trees by the creek to make a swing. We approached them and got the lowdown on what was happening in town, like the dog that got hit by the grain truck and the brush fire along the railroad tracks. Finally I asked, "How would you guys like to come with Mike and me? Sure would like you to see this strange machine we found."

"Machine?" Jeff asked, "What kind of machine?" We described the ship and the men. Mike got all excited, now that he had the chance to tell some kids about the ship. He didn't talk much to Mr. Brooks, who liked to talk about the grain market, politics, and the War, and didn't worry very much about the men in the spaceship.

"It is round and great big," he affirmed in his best English, holding his arms out like he was hugging a fat lady. "Big like a barn. Round like a dollar with colored lights on the sides. It flies through the sky." He went on talking about the ship, how it didn't make any sound at all and how the men wore clothes that looked like uniforms. They were all looking at him like he was talking about breeding jackrabbits with carp to get turkeys.

"Leo," Jeff asked me, apparently deciding that Mike had too much sun, "where is this machine now?"

"Up in the hills about a mile and a half from our place," I replied. I felt like we might have some success with them, even if they were just going to prove us wrong. "We've seen it three times now. Do you want to come with us today?"

"How many times have you been up there?" one of the other kids asked.

"We been there dozens of times," Mike piped up before I could stop him. That did it right there. I knew that I had lost the sale.

"You been there dozens of times and only seen it three times?"

"Well, yeah, but it's really something. You never seen anything like it in your life." The day was a hot one, so I wasn't surprised when Jeff answered.

"I don't want to hike that far—not on a hot day like this. You other guys want to go, you can, but I'm not. I think we can get an old piece of rope at the stockyard. Let's go down there and look." The group of boys moved off with Jeff and left Mike and me looking at each other.

I guess they were all scared or thought that we were crazy to go up and sit on that hill in the sun, waiting for some kind of ship to fly in and land. We would not give up. This was something we had to do. Part of the problem was that my folks were German. We more often spoke German around the house than English. There was a lot of prejudice in the years after the War and we had two strikes against us. We were both German and Catholic. There were many prejudices and a lot of hatred between people of different religions at that time as well. They called us "Sauerkraut Eaters," "Catholicers," "Fish Eaters," and other things I will not repeat. They were right about the fish, though. If we went fishing and all we caught were suckers, we ate the suckers. They said Jews were greedy and were supposed to be keeping all the money so there was none for the rest of us. During those times, any kid who talked with an accent or whose parents came from a foreign country was called a "foreigner" and nasty remarks were made. The town kids all stuck together and we lived far enough out that we didn't have much of anyone to stick together with but each other. Whatever the reason, nobody ever went with us to see the spaceship.

A couple of days later, we headed out to the valley in the evening after chores, just before dusk. This was around the end of August 1932, and the days were still quite long. The sunset came around eight-thirty and we had a couple of hours of good light left. To our joy, our ship slowly settled itself down to the ground. Our determination was rewarded and we were witnessing the whole thing. This time, however, we had accomplished something new. We were a little closer than before, sitting farther down the hill in the deepening shadows. As the ship approached the ground, we found ourselves immersed in the invisible field of force. It came over us like a flood of water that got thicker and thicker as the ship dropped lower and lower until we could not move.

This got quite interesting in a spooky sort of way. Always before, we couldn't get any closer. Now we couldn't get out. We were caught inside the shell of force and were unable to free ourselves, no matter how hard we tried to wiggle or strain. We struggled only briefly. It was clearly pointless to struggle and very easy to just sit and watch. I do not think I tried to speak to Mike. I did not have to. It was like we were thinking the same thing and both of us knew it. We were just sitting on the ground and watched the door open and the men appear again.

The door was so different from any doors we had ever seen, and it opened in such a very unusual way I have no words to describe it. It amazed and intrigued me, but then, I felt the door was proper and appropriate. Anything capable of traveling at such great speed, I reasoned, would have to be very complex. A spaceship wouldn't have doors like a barn or a Reo truck, it would have special spaceship doors. I found myself wishing Mr. Brooks had told us more about the zeppelin doors and longing to see the men walking around again before it got too dark. We were not actually frightened by our predicament, but were more excited and curious about the new sensations. It was like the time a train thundered by us only a foot or two away, only it was thoughts that were roaring through our minds.

We were sitting on a remote hillside more than a mile away from our home in growing darkness, caught in a strange force with no way to get out. It started to sink into my mind. We were unable to move in any direction. I noticed that Mike was scared and not scared like I was. Being locked in by this strange force threw us into a panic. We felt certain they had spotted us as they were landing, and we were quite sure they were watching us. Strangely, we felt we had somehow made them our friends, though we had never gotten closer to them than the length of a football field and were still shook up and a bit nervous about them. I think they were always aware of our presence from the very beginning and were doing something to calm and soothe us so that we would not be alarmed by the experience. There was another factor at work. Because we were brothers, we each tried to hide our fright from the other. We were all the time daring each other to do one thing or another, and bragging back and forth about who was the bravest. Maybe they were able to examine us more closely now that we were trapped in the force. The storm of thoughts and feelings was certainly like nothing we had ever experienced with them before.

Although Mr. Brooks was the only other person who said he believed us, it gave us great encouragement. Our earlier conversation with him replayed in my brain like the commercial jingles and tunes we heard in the evenings on the radio. If more people had believed us, I think we would have been more frightened. Everyone told us we had quite an imagination and we were seeing things that weren't there. On many days, I'm sure we halfway believed them. But now we couldn't deny it. How could our imaginations keep us motionless like we were sitting in grain bin, covered up to our eyeballs?

I remember two very strong images from that experience. One was an old buck antelope we often saw around the farm. One of his horns was bent, so we could always tell it was him. He knew us and we knew him. I guess he decided we were harmless, because he let his does and fawns graze as we walked by, but he was always watching us. He was our friend in a similar way to these strange visitors. They watched us like that old antelope.

The other image was our old dog, who had tangled with a porcupine and got a nose full of quills. Dad got a pair of pliers and held the dog's head under his arm, while we handled the end that didn't bite. The dog struggled frantically at first, but then became quiet as Dad pulled the quills, one after the other. I as sure it hurt that old dog terribly, but he knew that we were trying to help him, and was willing to put up with just about anything to get rid of that painful mess in his nose. Our fear went away just like the dog's fear. Our minds were buzzing with thoughts and impressions.

We felt that we were now becoming a little bit closer to them, and on a much friendlier basis. If we could just keep this up, maybe we could even get into that ship. We were finally close enough to get a better look at these people. If they were from some other world, maybe they wanted to live here. Could this be the army or some manufacturer who was testing something?

We thought if we could get close enough to them, we might be able to talk with them. I knew this wouldn't be easy and I was a little scared to try it. On the outside I felt brave, but deep down I was still scared. If we could just get a little bit closer, just close enough to see what they really looked like—but they held us in their forces. We could not get any closer to them. We could not leave that spot. This put me in a slight panic again. I knew we had asked for this. I felt a little more at ease after thinking it over for a while.

We finally convinced ourselves that we probably had nothing to worry about. Deep down in our bones, we finally knew for sure we were not imagining it. We now felt we were into the real thing.

We just sat there keeping an eye on that ship. They had come here for some other reason than just advertising. Here we were, trapped maybe two or three hundred feet from the ship, fighting our feelings of panic. I wish I could adequately convey the way we were rapidly alternating from feelings of fear to safety, from doubt to curiosity, from wonderment to speculation. The great intensity of the experience is very memorable to me today.

I'm sure they were aware of us even if they did ignore us. They probably felt that if they did look at us, we would get scared and something might happen to us. Mike and I didn't feel like we knew what was going through their minds, but we surely did a lot of guessing about it. Many times I have wished we could have realized then, while it was happening, that we were dealing with very highly intelligent beings beyond our capabilities of thinking or understanding.

This was during the tough times of drought and I felt they might be checking our vegetation. They gave us the feeling that they were very interested in what was happening with the plants and creatures in the countryside. These impressions were entering our minds just like our own thoughts, peaceful and friendly, offering no threat at all.

"I'm beginning to wonder what is happening on this planet," my brother said. I knew it was him, that little kid sitting next to me, that was sending these thoughts to me. He usually wondered about things like what had happened to one of his toys, or if he would get to ride in the truck with Dad to town. Here he was concerned about our planet. A month ago he didn't even know what a planet was. Neither did I. What was happening to us?

Putting two and two together with the dry years and the crop failures and the pests, we felt there had to be some connection with the purposes of these visitors and their fantastic ship.

We had asked several other people besides Mr. Brooks if they had ever seen one of these ships. We felt that some of them had, but they were afraid to say anything. Maybe other people had told them to forget about it because no one would believe them. This was actually what we were facing, what we were thinking, what they were "picking up" from our thoughts. We didn't understand it all yet, but were still desperately determined to meet these people. Nothing disturbed our certainty that they would not harm us in any way, because we felt they knew we just wanted to be friends with them.

"We've got to get inside that ship," my brother said. "We have got to get close enough to hear what they're talking about. Their mouths are moving, but we can't hear what they're saying."

Mike and I could see all this. It was so dark I couldn't see my hands or feet in front of me or the bushes around us, but we could see their hands moving hundreds of feet away from us. How could this be happening? We hadn't a clue, but we still couldn't get close enough to them to see their faces distinctly. It did not strike us as unusual that we could see these things near the ship while we sat in darkness on the hillside.

We were now firmly convinced we were not just seeing things and were not just imagining this whole spaceship experience. We could talk and breathe easily, but we could not move our limbs. Then, somewhere in the depths of my kid brain, the thought came bubbling up that Mom and Dad were going to skin us alive for staying out so late. Though we often went on hunting expeditions that lasted after dark, Mom would get worried about us when we didn't tell here in advance we would be home late.

"Mike," I said, "we are dealing with the real thing—something that really exists and comes from another world, but we are going to be in serious trouble when we get home late tonight."

Just like that, my foot gave way and I kind of slipped sideways and rolled to the ground. We had been released from the force that was holding us. As soon as we found ourselves free, we didn't stick around to see anything more. We just headed straight for home in the now almost complete darkness. This was the first time we left feeling we should. A city kid might be nervous about walking around in those dark hills without a light, but we were country kids and could find our way by the starlight. We used the few lights toward town, the Fleck Place, and our own farm as navigation beacons.

On our way home we decided not to tell our dad what happened this time because he would say something like, "I guess I don't have enough for you boys to do. You are just dreaming foolishness." Believe me, we had plenty of chores to do. Mike and I were both surprised by our reception at home that night. Our parents were not worried about us and there were no embarrassing questions to answer. I think Dad got a big payment on a job he was doing for someone. That was always cause for good feelings at home, but it never seemed to happen often enough.

I think it was at this point that our attitude toward our experiences started to change. We began to keep more to ourselves on the subject of the ship, just Mike and I talking about it to each other when we were alone. We began to keep our thoughts more to ourselves as the many new ideas percolated through our minds and we tried to understand it all.

It was three days later, on August 28, around eight in the evening before we were able to return to the valley. I remember that three days remained in the month because Dad had received another cash payment and things were happy again at home. We topped the hill at a run and eagerly looked down into the valley to see our ship sitting on the same spot as before.

As we approached the ship, moving carefully down the brushy, uneven hillside, we could see them moving about, strangely illuminated in the growing shadows. We again found ourselves blocked by that invisible force, but we were now far closer than we'd ever been. By this time, we had concluded the barrier was like a magnetic force that affected people and animals instead of iron and steel. Now that we found ourselves so much closer to the ship, we could hardly contain our excitement. These people were being very cautious with us. It was our best chance yet to see them up close, but sundown was coming on fast. Discounting their clothing, they looked very much like someone you might see walking around Bismarck.

"They all look the same," Mike whispered. "There are six of them." It was true. They were all about the same build and the same size, between five and six feet tall, and all wore a similar light coverall or jumpsuit. I thought to myself how great I would look in their clothing.

"It looks like they are all men, doesn't it? No women with long hair or—" he gestured at his chest.

"Yeah. None of 'em look like women, but none of them look very burly, either. I don't they'd last very long on a thrashing crew." We were used to comparing strangers to the hands on Dad's thrashing crew, many of whom could break a two-by-four like a matchstick.

"Do you think they will let us in the ship, Leo? Do you think they're getting rocks?" The men near the ship often bent down, seeming to touch the ground with their hands. We were still not close enough to see much detail, maybe thirty or forty feet away from the nearest one of them.

"They are our friends, aren't they Leo? They know we can't hurt them, don't they Leo?" He was waving at them shyly, but they didn't seem to be giving us any attention at all. He started tugging on my shirt. "Leo, Leo, they can see us can't they?"

"Of course they can see us. Don't rip my shirt off of my back. Maybe they don't wave at people like we do." I couldn't even begin to answer his questions. He wasn't even this excited at Christmas. When he was small, I thought he would never start talking. Now it was like he could not stop. I found myself wishing he could get his answers from them.

"We can make friends with them, can't we Leo?" Mom and Dad were always watching who we were friendly with and wouldn't let us associate with some kids at all. What was the harm in trying to make friends with them? After all, nobody believed they were here. Nobody beside them would know what we saw or did there. Maybe they would give us some money like the field hands sometime did when they got paid.

"Leo, we have to talk to them and find out why they are here." He started calling out louder and louder and began waving his arms, but they only continued their odd behavior and ignored us. Then, before I knew what was happening, he started jumping up and down, yelling, and shaking the bushes. That did it. Several of them were looking directly at us now. I wanted to thump him on the head. We found ourselves enveloped again by that silent, invisible wave that locked us into place. Mike's curiosity was like a live animal running around inside him all the time. When we were doing chores, he drew pictures of the ship in the dirt at every opportunity and asked me foolish questions about what was inside that ship and what the men were doing here. He was right there with me every time I saw them and we both knew he'd seen everything I had. How could I tell him anything about that ship that he didn't already know?

"Well, Mike, I hope you are happy now. They have us stuck like a cow in a mudhole again. Do you see what your foolishness has done for us now?"

"At least they know we're here," he said stubbornly. He shut up after that, though. I think it scared him a little. Maybe they thought all his excited shouting and movements would attract attention, or maybe he was just annoying them. Whatever the reason, it was again up to them to release us.

The torrent of strange thoughts and impressions had returned, mingled with many questions that were unmistakably our own, mostly centering on why the men all looked so much alike. Their similarity was something more than the way members of a single family all kind of look alike. The men must have all been about the same age, which seemed to be younger than Dad, and were all smooth-faced, with no sign of beard or moustache.

"They are still our friends," Mike whispered confidently. "They would let their friends inside, wouldn't they, Leo?" It often seemed to us that we didn't have any friends at all in town. After some of the things they said and did, Jeff and the others sometimes seemed more like enemies than friends. Then Mike said something that made me think.

"We can have friends that come from another galaxy because they're foreigners too."

"I don't think we will have any problems," I allowed, "since we can't hurt them. We will probably worry about how to get back out if they let us in. Don't ever let Dad hear you call us 'foreigners,' Mike. We are Americans, just like everybody else around here."

"They are not Americans," he countered, looking at the men. He had me there. I had to agree that I didn't think they were Americans. Maybe they were Canadians, though most of the Canadians we had seen looked like ordinary North Dakota Americans to us.

The sun had settled below the horizon before the men returned to their ship and it disappeared into the evening sky with the faint humming vibration and the same spectacular display of brilliant colored lights we remembered from before. We were able to move away from the valley only after the ship had left. I looked up into the clear sky as we walked home and saw a triangle of three bright stars, overhead and to the east. Were these men from one of those stars?

When we arrived home that night, Dad was working on the engine of one of the trucks and Mom was holding the lantern for him. He had been gone to Bismarck when we left that afternoon. The mechanic work now was a sure sign that the money had gone into parts instead of into new clothes or shoes for us and Mom. We went right to bed to avoid questions from them about why we were so late. We had plenty of questions of our own that we could not answer. Why did these men all look so much alike? Mike and I were brothers and we didn't look that much alike. Why didn't the men call back to us? Why did they let us approach so near this time and then stop us in our tracks? How could they produce a "magnetic" force that affected people the way magnets repel each other? Were they really from some other galaxy or just government test pilots from Canada? Mr. Brooks had told us exciting stories about test pilots who would fly any kind of strange contraption the government could dream up, sometimes straight into the ground.

I fell asleep plugging away at these thoughts. We had never heard about a galaxy before in our lives, but it did not seem strange to me to be thinking about distant galaxies as I lay there in my bed. I did not know for sure what a galaxy was, but I knew it was away up in the sky. I thought about those three bright stars we saw and wondered if they were galaxies or just regular old stars. I wondered if living on a galaxy was like living on a star and if it was as big as Bismarck or Minot or Minneapolis. It did not strike me as unusual that, although it was quite dark when we finally stumbled back up the hill and headed for home, we could always clearly see the men moving about their ship.

We tried again on the twenty-ninth, leaving home before sunrise at about six-thirty in the morning and arriving at the valley as the sun came up. We saw no ship. The three bright stars I remembered from overhead in the evening sky were gone. The few remaining stars were mostly in the east, and soon disappeared in the rising sun. Again we walked down into the valley to examine the spot that had been the site of so much interesting activity the night before. We felt they should have pushed the grass down and left tracks where they had been walking, but we found they didn't seem to leave any markings at all. Nothing was left on the ground, not a trace of water or anything.

When the thrash crew left an area where they had worked for several days, there was always a great deal of rubbish left everywhere—cigarette and cigar butts, scraps of paper and uneaten lunches, discarded items of clothing, piles of manure, and dirty rags. The thrash machine, grain trucks, and the horses pulling their heavy wagons always left very noticeable tracks. These men left nothing at all that we could discover. We even had a spirited argument about the kind of garbage they would produce. Mike thought they might leave egg shells or wet spots where they dumped out wash water and such, but we saw nothing.

We thought their months and days and time keeping might be different from ours and decided to go back home and try again in the afternoon. We hiked back to the spot in the early afternoon, but saw nothing out of the ordinary. No ship again. For some reason, I told Mike we should hang around for a while and he agreed. After we spent only a short time on the hilltop, our ship approached. We could not understand how, but we felt they had some way they could land the ship and depart again without being seen. We had experienced this before. When we watched them take off, the minute they got a few feet above the ground, we lost sight of them. They were just gone. The feeling was growing in us that, like a baseball struck by a bat, they were instantly moving so fast that they were just invisible to us. We thought if they could move out that quickly, they could certainly slow their ship just as quickly.

As we tried to approach the ship, we were blocked by their "magnetic" force while we were still very near the hilltop. This bothered Mike. He worried that they might have lost some confidence in us because of the way he acted the previous night. They did not want us any closer, but again, we finally managed to draw their attention. They raised their hands toward us and then mostly ignored us. We knew then we were making some headway with them, and Mike began to feel a little better about it. Would we get to meet them? How would we ever get to talk to them? We were still a little bit scared and debated why we really wanted to meet them.

"Things are too tough around here anyway," my brother said. "Maybe they would take us where life is better. That would be something to see, Leo." I didn't know what he was thinking about. Why would these people want a couple of dumb kids in their way all the time? Mike would last about a day away from Mom and then he would start crying to go home.

He was even like that when we went to stay with our grandparents. Mike always got homesick.

In the meantime, we had reached a decision about their home, and answered the question within our own minds as to whether they were from our world or actually from some other galaxy. Without quite knowing why, we had dismissed our own world and now definitely felt they came from a distant galaxy, perhaps one of the very stars we saw that morning or the night before.

As we stood watching them and speculating to each other about them, we could feel them looking us over, examining us in some way I could not quite define. We felt they were definitely interested in us in a friendly way.

"We either got ourselves into trouble," Mike said, "or we are going to talk to them. Nobody believes us. If they take us with them, no one will miss us at all." Mike was not giving our parents much credit.

"Well, don't you go raising a fuss again, Mike, or next thing you know, they will run us off." It was kind of exasperating for us just sitting around there in the sun and watching them perform the strange exercises that didn't make any sense to us. Whatever it was they were doing, they were very busy about it, coming and going from the ship with small parcels and odd gadgets we couldn't quite see. There could have been dozens of them inside, but we never saw more than six of them outside at one time. As before, they all wore similar clothing, the coveralls I admired.

"They don't have any buttons, Leo." Mike was right. There were no visible buttons or even a seam in front that might be hiding the buttons. I was guessing to myself how they might get in and out of such garments when I realized the shoes were not separate from the trousers. The clothing was similar to the sleepers that our little brother wore in bed.

Mike was simply a fountain of questions. "What's he doing? What is he carrying? Why is that fellow looking at the bushes?" It was "why this?" and "what is that?" nonstop.

We were still a little scared, but they showed a friendly attitude toward us. We talked this over between us and decided we might soon have a chance to get into their ship. If we could accomplish this, we would see things no one else in Killdeer had ever seen. This was our next step. We had a feeling that chance would come soon. Looking back, I am sure they were just observing our behavior as they held us at arm's length and completed their tasks. Their activity all seemed too closely coordinated. After a time, the activity near the ship died down until only one of them remained outside, wandering here and there with no pattern. He came quite close to us, maybe ten or twelve feet away. Whatever was holding us seemed to have no effect upon him. He looked directly at us and smiled in a peaceful and friendly way, raising his hand with the open palm toward us. Then he turned and walked directly back to the ramp and entered the ship. Although the ramp retracted into the ship and the strange door closed, nothing else happened. It was as though they were digesting the results of all their activities.

After the door closed, we were released. We decided not to try to go up to the ship, though it was very tempting to touch it. We wanted to impress them that we were on our best behavior and would not upset any of their projects that might still be underway. It seemed like we had been there for several hours, but the sun was still hanging low in the west when we left. Heading for home, we agreed not to talk about our adventure with anyone. This time we were definitely late for supper.

Our supper was on the table when we arrived. We were having soup, fresh beans, pork, and mashed potatoes. Supper looked good, but we were so involved in our latest experience that we were not very hungry. It was just one of those things—we were just too involved. There was no thought of mentioning what happened to us that night. Our parents still thought we were imagining all these things and Mom was unhappy and worried because we did not eat. As far as she was concerned, something was wrong when we weren't hungry. We both knew the big thing left to do was to find some way to prove it to our parents and everybody else—somehow. But there was no way to do it.

The excitement was starting to build up in us because, deep down, we felt our ship would be back the next night, and somehow, if we could get there, we could probably get much closer to them. If they were intelligent enough to get here from another world or another galaxy, we figured they could travel from one galaxy to another whenever they wanted. Though we were not educated enough to understand such things, we had all these thoughts about other galaxies, which we pictured as huge, distant cities like New York and Paris and London. Everything about these travelers was so different from the people we knew. Their home simply had to be on another world far away.

Since nobody in town but Mr. Brooks believed us and we had decided to keep our experiences to ourselves, we arrived at these conclusions between each other mostly without comments or observations from any other people. It was our own experiences that made us feel this way, not someone feeding us outlandish stories. We also noticed these people were very healthy and prosperous looking. We felt they must eat much better than anybody in this surrounding area and didn't lack anything they might need or want. Of course, this was during the depression days when things were tough and everyone was looking for any kind of advantage just to survive.

An incident that happened in town might have had something to do with us keeping our exploits in the valley to ourselves. There was a man in Killdeer who bought and sold chickens. He had some wire pens where he kept the chickens before he shipped them. Mike and I were walking by the pens one day and saw a chicken outside the pen pecking busily away in the brush. We chased that little rooster into a corner and caught him in short order. I had the frightened bird under my arm when we walked into the building where the man was working to return his chicken. He was very pleased with us and gave us each a dime for our help! He said anytime we found a chicken loose outside the pens, he would reward us for returning it.

You can bet we studied the entire chicken layout very closely after that, but the chickens were not persistent enough about making good their escape to keep us in movie money. We found the place where the wire had come, apart allowing the birds to squeeze out. Mike was small enough to worm his way into the bushes and try to fix the opening, but it just seemed to get worse. After that, we would make as much as a dollar in a good week. The chicken man started looking at us funny when we returned his chickens and business suddenly fell off drastically. Mike crawled back in to see what was wrong, and then wiggled back out with a long look on his face.

"It's all new wire, Leo. We're out of luck." When we emerged from the brush behind the pens, we saw the chicken man watching us with a funny look on his face and just headed back home.

It was at night, as I tried to get to sleep, that my mind buzzed even more than ever with excited thoughts and questions about the visitors. I had begun to have a growing feeling that the men from the spaceship were affecting me and Mike in some way I could not quite put my finger on. It was not a scary or threatening feeling and was very tough to pin down or prove in a way that would satisfy a scientist.

When we walked out to the valley, that "something" in the back of my mind told me whether they were going to be there or not. Somehow, I could not quite get myself to believe it without actually going there to look. We always left the valley with the feeling we would have to come back once more without talking to them. Some kind of an attachment toward them was developing in us. They were drawing us back by feeding our curiosity, just like spilled grain draws the chickens. We did not seem to have any other alternative, but liked it to be that way. These were the kinds of thoughts that ran through my mind. I would later become convinced they were penetrating our minds and knew what we were thinking, but back then I just had the growing feeling that they were friendly and knew everything about us. We were always so nervous and excited each time we saw them that we were ready to run like jackrabbits. I began to see they could sense our fears and were keeping us at a distance to allow us to grow used to them and overcome our fears.

When I think back now, I know their huge ship was the key to our interest in them. As individuals, they were not all that much different from ordinary people. If you dressed them in ordinary clothing, you would pass one of them in a strange town without blinking an eye. We were quite convinced that if they could build and fly this amazing airship, they could do many other exciting things we could only imagine. By now, we had begun to suspect they could control the weather, because the conditions were always calm and clear each time they landed. It was always strictly peaceful and quiet when the ship was in the valley. There was never a breeze or a wind of any kind. Mike and I got to imagining what they could do with the weather one day while we were swimming. We were actually wading around in one of the deep spots in the Killdeer River that always held some water, even when most of the river had dried up in the summer heat. The water was cold and deep enough so we could sit on the muddy bottom with the water up to our noses.

"I bet they could make a tornado come through and suck all the water out of this swimming hole," I said when we bobbed to the surface like a couple of frogs. It was fun watching Mike's eyes get wide, just like a frog's eyes. "But they wouldn't." I could tell that Mike liked the idea of a tornado that could drain a pond into the sky.

"Why not? Maybe they need the water for their radiator." As the sons of a man who ran a thrasher as well as grain and gravel trucks, we knew more about machinery than many of our farm friends who seldom saw anything more complicated than a team of horses and a wagon. We had watched Dad probing the insides of carburetors and magnetos and had shocked ourselves silly with ignition spark coils. Mike was certain the ship must have engines similar to the huge new Reo grain truck we had seen when we went on a trip to Bismarck with our father to get parts.

"They wouldn't want dirty old pond water for that ship." I wasn't sure if the ship had a radiator or not, but I didn't want Mike to know that I didn't know. "They wouldn't take it anyway because they are our friends and wouldn't spoil our swimming hole for us." Our pool had snakes, frogs, dragonflies, horseflies, mosquitoes, and even small brown leeches that made great bait and would cling to our feet and legs after we left the water. It was always a sure escape from the endless summer heat. It was one of the big attractions in our life, next to the ship.

I knew that one day we would come into closer contact with them, but did not know if we would ever be allowed to enter that spaceship. That was the goal for us, to get inside that ship. We were pretty sure they wouldn't hurt us, but would they take us seriously and not treat us like foolish kids who are just in the way? Maybe they would let us pass the tools to them when they worked on the engine like our father did. If only we could approach close enough to talk to them. But, would they know our language? If they did not know our language, how could we possibly ask to visit their ship? What if they only spoke Swedish and Norwegian and we couldn't ask them the hundreds of questions that were eating away at our imaginations? Would they speak English or German? How would we ever be able to satisfy our curiosity if we couldn't talk to them?

I reviewed the events we had experienced over and over again. We were quite scared when the strange force held us, but then in some mysterious way, we were always released unharmed. Something always told us to head straight for home so we wouldn't get in trouble with our parents. When we arrived home, we always felt we were getting ourselves deeper into what might be a serious situation. One day we got worried about being involved in something so serious without telling our parents all about it, so we again approached Mom and Dad. They finally agreed to sit down with us and listen to what we had to say. I am sure they noticed how we had developed knowledge they could not account for. They listened to our excited words, but watching them, I don't think they quite believed us. They were just pacifying us.

Mother saw more of us than Dad, so I guess she started to notice how our experiences with these visitors were changing us before our father did. She heard us arguing about stars and planets and galaxies, maybe not in those words, but the ideas were there. She began to wonder where we were getting these ideas. We had been playing in a pile of sand that Dad had dumped for us at the edge of the big yard, running our toy trucks through the sand pile intersection and loudly imitating the sounds made by the grinding gears, roaring engines, and cursing drivers. When Dad came home that night, Mother called him to look at the road and bridge pattern we had made in the sand during our play. Mike and I spied on them and heard her exclaim to him how our roads looked like a flower. I remember the pattern that impressed her—today we would recognize it a cloverleaf interchange on an interstate highway.

That night, Dad left the house after about ten minutes of our tale, saying he had to do his chores. Undaunted, we told our mother the most detailed version of our story so far. Mother listened to our fantastic tale, asking a question now and then, and finally said, "I have always believed that when you leave this world, there is a better world ahead. Maybe somewhere along the line you two kids have stumbled into something that no one understands. I know I don't understand it myself. But I believe that our world surely exists, our 'planet,' as you call it. There is no reason I can see why planets with people cannot also exist in some other place.

"We know that men are flying and fighting wars with airplanes. Why couldn't it be that you two kids saw this 'ship' by being in the right place at the right time? Maybe, by some act of God, you were meant to see this. Maybe you are part of it or are becoming part of it by what you have been doing. The only people that will ever know for sure will be you two. People will always doubt you. You must understand that, boys. You are going to have to live with it yourselves. You've got me pretty well convinced that you are not just coming home with wild stories anymore. It has gone way beyond that point because you have learned too many things. You talk about too many different things. There are so many things that you have learned that we have never talked about. Where do your words come from? Boys, you'll just have to explore it and satisfy your hearts and your minds. As soon as your minds are satisfied, you will know in your heart where you are and understand what you have seen—what you have learned. Although the world may not believe you now, maybe in the future, in the seventies or even the eighties, people will believe you. Many of us may not be here, but I am sure you boys will still be here."

From that point on, we took her growing belief for granted and developed more courage and determination. It was the thought that Mother, at least, was beginning to take us more seriously that finally enabled me to go to sleep that night. It helped on many other nights as well, when we went to bed with our disappointment at having seen nothing in the valley that day.

Another source of support could always be found at the elevator in town. We often headed back to talk with Mr. Brooks. Finding him alone was not too hard in those drought times, so we were often able to discuss our experiences with him.

After hearing our excited rendition of the latest events in the valley, Mr. Brooks said, "Boys, if you have gone this far, then for your own peace of mind you've got to see it through." His encouragement and confirmation of our sightings along with Mom's growing acceptance of our unusual behavior, kept us going on the many trips to the valley when we saw nothing at all. We swallowed our disappointment on those occasions and slowly learned to listen to that subtle inner voice that pointed out the pattern to their appearances. Evenings were always the best. Our next successful contact came late in the afternoon after an unsuccessful try that same morning.

When we arrived on the crest of the hill, we saw the ship in its usual location and found the people outside and moving around aimlessly, almost as though they were exercising. They would bend down to the ground and seemingly picked up something. This gave us a strange feeling they were doing this same "exercise" all over the world, not just here in our countryside. Mike and I just assumed they were landing all over those Killdeer Mountains. We assumed that this one machine covered our entire planet. We were convinced it was fast enough to do just that. Why did these convictions grow in our minds, just from seeing them moving about near their ship? Did these thoughts, which we believed were our own, actually come from them?

We were still more determined to get close enough to that machine to speak to these people and find out what they were doing and how they were surviving the tough times in so much apparent comfort. These strangers seemed to be much smarter and healthier than either of us or anyone else we knew. They had such fine clothing and footwear, such a splendid ship, so many things we didn't have. Down in our hearts, we felt that if we could see all the wonderful things that must be inside the ship, we could become part of it, at least in our minds. Our lives would be somehow improved. Since no one would believe us, we were not doing it to show off in front of others.

It was about 6:15 in the evening. We wanted to get inside that ship more than anything you can imagine, more, even, than eating supper.

As we started down the hill, we found ourselves in quite a different situation than before. The magnetic force they used to keep us at a distance was behind us and we were free to walk cautiously up toward the landing site. As we approached the ship, these people were outside with smiles on their faces. They were very calm, not in the least excited or nervous. They just went about their exercises and made us feel welcome, like we weren't in the way.

We stopped our approach at maybe eight or ten feet from the nearest of them, and just stood there watching. Our experiences with the thrashing crew had taught us not to approach their work area too closely, or risk a profane scolding from an angry worker who didn't want to lose his job for killing one of us. We just kind of stood there watching, ready to run if they yelled at us or started up some kind of frightening machine. We could hear no sounds in the strange stillness so near the tremendous ship. This close, we were nearly overwhelmed by its huge dimensions. I was so impressed by the ship that I was almost startled by my first close look at one of them.

These men were so ordinary looking in one way and so exotic in another. I noticed that they had light brown hair that was cut much the same as Mom cut ours. Their complexion was very light beige, resembling a good tan. Their eyes were blue with a dark pupil. I would guess their weight to be about 140 pounds, since they were a little taller and more heavily built than my father. He never weighed more than 130 pounds in his life. All of them looked to me to weigh about the same and be about the same size and build. They were very different from the husky farmers and field hands we were used to seeing. Their hands and feet were shaped like ours, but their shoes were totally unlike our own. Footwear without laces or a sole that was different from the tops we'd never seen before.

They wore different clothing from the last time we saw them. A top with slacks uniform replaced the coverall they had always worn before. The fabric of their clothing was very unusual, with a subtle pattern visible only when the light was just right. The color and cut of the uniform was the same from a distance, but that subtle pattern was different from one to another of them. Their otherwise identical uniforms looked like they were neatly pressed, but did not have badges or any other insignia that might show rank, like our soldiers did. We had seen real soldiers and sailors and were always thrilled by their colorful medals and stripes. I compared these men in my mind to the field hands, who came in every age, shape, and size, and who always wore a ragged assortment of work clothes. These men were as alike as peas in a pod.

Now that we were up close to it, we found the color of the ship to be a light blue that blended smoothly into the color of the sky. When viewed against the sky, the ship was strangely difficult to detect, either close up or from a distance. There was sort of a haze to it. We just stood there and looked back and forth from the ship to the men. They occasionally looked at us and smiled, then continued with their exercises. I was able to talk German probably better than English at that time, although our tongues were tied and we just couldn't speak. There were three of them, and they stood there and looked at us. They appeared to be very relaxed with that unusual smile on their faces. Their smile was like ours, probably more gentle and relaxed than ours, maybe more gentle than any smile I have ever seen.

Mike finally worked up his courage and tried to talk to the closest of them, but they all just went about their "exercises" with that smile on their faces. I was not surprised that they did not speak to him. He was so excited he was talking in the mixture of German and English that we used in speaking to each other around the farm.

Two of the men walked back into the ship and another came out, walked over to us and said in German, "I can speak your language." Then he said in English, "We speak all languages of all people on your planet." I was thrilled. Here was another person who knew what a planet was.

I must admit, he spoke very good German, and English, without an accent passing from one language to the other. He spoke either language like he had spoken it all his life. This reinforced our belief that these people were highly intelligent. We asked them some questions, not very deep questions, because we felt curiously tongue-tied. I knew Mike had questions coming out his ears. We had meant to ask a million questions, but in the end, we asked very few. The conversation with him lasted for only a few minutes, us saying one word and him saying ten words to us. We didn't see any women among them. I noticed they were wearing thin, light-colored gloves. Mike and I were hanging pretty close together, touching each other for security. Although we were very excited, we felt no fear as we spoke to them. In some way, they showed that much feeling toward us. This we understood. But as time progressed, we found ourselves in a position we did not understand at all.

Deep down I felt I wanted to ask them to take us into their ship, but I couldn't get the words to come out. Finally, one of these men came real close to us and spoke in that perfect German. "Boys, you have had quite an experience with us. You have showed great determination in coming to visit us again and again. You have seen much, you have learned much, and you know more about us than most people in your world. No one will believe you when you tell them about us." He looked right at me, "Not until you are an old man. No matter what you tell them about us, they will still not believe you. In your own minds, you will always know the truth about what you have experienced and felt." Then he repeated it carefully in English.

He said, "We are very real and we are from another galaxy. We have traveled to your planet for over five thousand years. We are from a place far beyond your world by millions of years in time. We continue traveling to your planet because it is part of our responsibility. We are showing you a small part of what you can expect in the future. You cannot learn everything at one time without rest. You will see us again before long. In the meantime, you must go home and rest, because your minds are not big enough to learn everything as quickly as you would like. Remember, you must believe what you have seen and understand what you have learned, and try to understand that we are not here to hurt anyone." He did not repeat his words in English because he knew we understood the German.

I did not ask them any more questions and we did not get into the spaceship. For once, Mike didn't seem to have any more questions either. If they could read our minds, they knew everything we were thinking, every question we wanted to ask, but they didn't start spewing answers to the mess that was boiling around in our brains. When we wanted to know something, it was clear we had to be able to ask the right question before we could get any answers. He stood before us for a few seconds more with that gentle smile on his face, then turned and joined the others. I was more than ready to go home, but now we were still close enough to look everything over quite closely. We probably could have entered the ship and seen all those things we wanted to see, but we still felt scared, even after every assurance they would not hurt us.

I gained many strong new impressions from those few words with them. For instance, I was now certain that they were far older than anyone we had ever met before. I could see it in the eyes of the man who spoke to me, which had that long, deep, tunnel-like appearance I associated only with the very old among our own people. Somehow, I knew they were the eyes of people who had seen and understood a large amount of life over a very long time. I could feel that look of experience in the glances and smiles of the others as well. They had very old, wise eyes in bodies that appeared to be young and fit. I decided they must have far better methods to protect their health and must live in a much better environment than we do. They glowed with perfect health. They didn't seem to make mistakes, at least not what we usually think of as mistakes.

I also knew they deeply respected our Earth, which they treated like an important old building, instead of "outside" like we did. This was why they didn't leave rubbish about, why their area was always clean. Their garbage was disposed of without throwing it out in a pile like we did.

I was now firmly convinced that these travelers from the spaceship could definitely read our minds. They responded to the questions, thoughts, and desires in our minds, and in turn were able to place their own thoughts, intentions, and beliefs in our minds without using words to explain these things to us in detail.

I was now positive they were intergalactic travelers, and that our galaxy was tied to theirs in some way. Otherwise they would not be interested in us and would not spend their own lives making journeys so long that we cannot even imagine the time and distance. We stood beneath the very same vessel that had been built in another world, using materials and concepts we could not imagine, and had traveled the impossible distance from their home to ours, just like we might go to China or Brazil. It was beautiful, unlike any machine we had ever seen, any we could imagine. It appeared to be one single piece of material without individual component parts. The ramp and supports beneath the ship appeared to join to the body of the ship without a seam. It was huge, but seemed to have none of the "presence," that feeling of something "being there" that we associated with buildings or railroad cars. I had the distinct feeling that a field hand could probably move it if he could figure out how to get hold of it. Perhaps that was the reason they adjusted the weather at their landing site to be perfectly still.

Everything we saw and learned about them told us we were dealing with peaceful, highly intelligent beings. They are a wise and gentle race of people, in contrast with the warlike and impulsive folks who exist on this planet. I was now positive they are not here to harm us. Because of their long history and high level of development, they are supreme beings, like gods to us. They are somehow responsible for the well-being of our planet. This is fortunate for humanity, because if they were hostile they certainly would have all they needed to make short work of us, and could have done so at any time throughout our short history. In our later years, Mike and I both came to realize that mankind will eventually learn they exist, and hoped that no rash bureaucrat would condemn them or try to destroy or capture them. I would fear for the safety of any attackers, if these visitors from space were forced to protect themselves. I was convinced that they had something in their ship that could have a tremendous impact if used as a weapon.

It seemed impossible that we had finally spoken to one of them and now stood so near the ship, which symbolized their existence to us. Our situation was nothing short of incredible. These people could travel safely from another galaxy, over a tremendous distance, and in a way impossible for the best of our science and technology. Yet here they were moving about near us in their calm and peaceful way, examining the earth beneath their ship. I felt at that time we were becoming part of them. We had not done much talking to them, but they had talked to us quite a lot. When we were with them, we were just quiet and a little bit scared, but our spirits were lifted and our hearts were stirred by the thought that we had finally made good contact with them. The assurance that we would be speaking with them again in the future helped a lot.

You may think that we wasted our first opportunity to learn something from them. That may be true. We were frustrated at our inability to speak to them at greater length, to ask all those questions that had been building up in our minds. When you just walk up to somebody from another world, another galaxy, a person who knows what you are thinking, it is confusing, almost impossible for you to ever open your mouth. You know that they are thinking everything you are thinking, that they already know the questions you want to ask before you can even open your mouth and find the words to ask. The answers to those questions are all mixed in as well. They were somehow able to fill up our minds with their presence and open a window into a world we could only dimly understand. People have told us over and over that we were crazy then and are crazy now when we describe what happened. I do not call it crazy, and I am certain that none of the time we spent with them was ever wasted.

All these questions and concerns did not worry us very much as we stood there gawking at them and their ship, but we were growing more overwhelmed and speechless and needed time to think about it. Of course they already knew this and what we wanted to do. They knew we did not want to harm them—all the odds were in their favor, anyway. The big thing that was in our favor was that we had learned something and experienced something that we could believe in. I believe that while we were with them, we were able to see what the future might hold. They told us that there is another galaxy where advanced people are living and that we are in some way a part of it. Otherwise, they would not spend their time and effort visiting this planet. There is definitely a purpose for them being here, and of course this was one of those things we were going to ask them.

There were so many things we wanted to do and to ask them. Somehow, we wanted to have a longer talk with them, but were tongue-tied. Our youthful brains were too flushed with the reality and thoughts of another civilization to operate. We were just itching to be able to touch their spaceship. All this was right there in front of us, yet we seemed to be unable to open our mouths or even to move our legs. At last, we had managed to meet them and build a closeness to them. I knew that the next time we would get even closer. Finally we mumbled "thank you" to them and they all gave us that peaceful smile. I told them we had to get home. One of them looked at us quite seriously and said, "Yes—yes you do."

Although we finally had our chance to explore something that we had been itching about for weeks, we couldn't manage to ask any more questions. How could we explain this? We couldn't. I guess it was just human nature. We were dealing with an intelligence farther beyond us than we were beyond our baby brother. What does a baby know about farming? How can a baby ask how a thrash machine works? There was no way in the world I could ask them a question that would make any sense. We encountered these things as kids, so we did not respond to them as we would have if we were adults. I have often wondered if we would have even had these experiences if we had been older. Maybe they looked at us as we might look at wild animals, which are easier to tame when very young, but sometimes grow up to be too dangerous or difficult to handle.

Mike and I started directly for home, cutting across the bottom of the valley and skirting our hillside. It was kind of downhill and brushy as we moved from the ship across the valley toward home. I think we fell a few times. Our heads were foggy and dazed, and I think we fell a few times. Our trips home were usually filled with excited discussions and arguments, but this time I do not remember talking. We kept our mouths shut when we got home and did not say anything about what had happened.

When we showed up at home and were cleaning up for supper, I think Mom must have noticed a difference in us. Every time she asked if we had seen anything interesting in our travels, we just said "Naw, nothing, just the same old thing."

Then our dad said, "I'm glad you are getting this thing out of your heads." Mike couldn't resist a small grin at that, which Mom saw, but Dad didn't seem to notice. I guess he had enough other things on his mind, because he talked mostly about business and politics. There was no mention about the harvest.

"The world is in a terrible mess," he said with a sad frown on his face. "As bad as it seems to be here, we are lucky we do not live in Germany." He went on to describe how bad people called "Nazis" were taking over Germany and how another war was brewing. "It is only a matter of time," he said, sadly shaking his head. "Before the killing will begin again. The Nazis cannot and will not pay reparations. They must steal what they need to rebuild Germany, because there is no money, not here and not in the old country." Reparations were large sums of money that the winners of the War decided the losers must pay to them as a form of punishment.

He and Mother talked about other bad people called "gangsters" who were killing each other in a place called Chicago because of moonshine alcohol. We were living in the last year of a time called "Prohibition," which had been in force for all the years of our lives. The law of that time prohibited people from selling beer, wine, whiskey, or any other drinks that contained alcohol. The gangsters were criminals who always had a lot of money because they sold alcohol. They drove around in powerful new automobiles, carried weapons like machine guns and pistols and sold alcohol in illegal saloons called "speakeasies."

The stories about the gangsters who sold alcohol always puzzled me because the people around Killdeer who sold alcohol were not at all like the gangsters we heard about. We had several "moonshiners" around Killdeer. They were just farmers who made alcohol in hidden spots out in the hills to help make ends meet and help feed their families. I had even worked for one of them the year before, keeping the fire burning beneath the still burning while he was out working in his fields.

Something just kept telling me not to say more. They were still talking about gangsters when we left the table and carried the scraps out to the dog. Even though our heads were still spinning from this first real contact with the visitors, we wanted more. We were already planning in whispers for our next meeting with our new friends, which we were certain would come within the next few days. Nothing could be allowed to block our efforts to get inside that ship. If Dad should devise some new work project to divert our imaginations from "foolishness," we might find ourselves too busy or too played out to get away for a trip to the valley.

It seemed that most of our efforts to involve others in our discovery brought us only problems. The town boys didn't need any additional excuses to make life difficult for a couple of "Krauts" who told fantastic stories about impossible events in their odd-sounding speech. Mr. Brooks was busy and, anyway, was always more interested in talking politics and telling his own stories than he was in listening to ours.

Several more days went by. My brother and I were bursting with our new experience and were arguing and discussing our decision not to tell anybody about what had happened to us this time. We had not given up on trying to figure out a way that someone might believe us. Try as we would, we could not understand why no one really cared or was willing to take a chance to learn so much about our future. In the end, we found it was easiest to get ever more tight-mouthed about our experiences. We finally began to realize that we were learning more from a short visit with these people than we could learn in ten of our school.

The following days were busy, and it seemed something always came up to prevent us from returning to the valley. I think Dad started working on a project that took him away from home and Mike and I had to stick close to the farm and help Mom as much as we could.

* * * * * *

Late in the day on September 19, kind of on the spur of the moment, we decided to go back to the valley. We were walking across the yard toward the barn after supper and knew that if Dad saw us hanging around, he'd put us to work. Mike looked at me and asked, "Do you think they are out there now?"

"I guess we can't tell from here," I responded, "can we?" Just like that, we changed our direction from the barn toward the Fleck place and the valley beyond. We waved at Mom, who was watching us from the kitchen window.

"Mom knows where we're going, doesn't she?"

"There's not much that she doesn't know about us, Mike." I grabbed a stick I'd left leaning against a fence post and began stabbing the air with it like it was a cavalry saber. Mike found a stick of his own and we fought a running battle all across the Fleck place, slapping our legs with our free hands to add extra hoof beats as we galloped. One moment we were attacking the Indians, slashing and shooting. Then the tide of the battle would change and the Indians would strike back or a German machine gun would cut loose from a hidden pillbox. Our imaginations, fueled by tales of the Indian wars and the great European battles, were not bothered that our opponents came from different continents and different centuries. After all, we were on our way to see the spaceship that came from a different world.

Although we felt that we might have to make two or three or a dozen more trips over those hills before we could get into that spaceship, we knew this might be our lucky day. The feeling that we were dealing with intelligent adults who expressed their warm feelings toward us and welcomed our visits gave us a tremendous sense of belonging. We knew that we would be welcome when we saw them again. This was one of the feelings we discovered in the three days following that first meeting.

We arrived back at the valley just after sundown to find the spaceship waiting there once again. Our movements were not blocked by the magnetic force. We could cross through their force field and freely approach their spaceship. I do not know why, but I had the impression that the force field was still there, but they "tuned" it somehow to allow us to pass through. Though we could see none of them outside on the ground, we felt they knew we had crossed through their magnetic force and were "knocking on their door." They were probably watching us walk toward their ship and made an opening in their beam to allow us to pass. After all those weeks and all those trips to the valley, our interest was still mainly focused on trying to see what that ship looked like inside. This time, we decided we would at least try to touch it, or maybe to touch one of those people. We did not simply stroll right up close to it, but would take a few steps closer and then stop and gawk for a while before moving on.

The ship was so awesome to us because it didn't behave at all like the ordinary objects we were accustomed to. While the men seemed very much like ordinary people, the ship was different. It definitely was not an ordinary thing. The men we respected, but their ship awed us. Offering a description of that ship is a difficult task. It was different from ordinary objects in so many ways. I could not understand those differences at the time, and can only speculate about them now that I have thought it over for many years.

I have mentioned how the ship did not have the "presence" of a building or a hillside. For another thing, it did not reflect light like ordinary objects. Rather, it seemed to absorb the light around it and produce its own subtle light of any color or pattern of shades they wished, like the chameleon. Sounds did not echo off it like the wall of a barn or the face of a cliff. You could stand right next to it and not even notice it was there. I think you might walk right by it if they didn't want you to be aware of it. It was more like a living thing that watched and reacted to its surroundings, than a machine or a building that just sat there.

Maybe they were putting on a show for us, because the appearance of the ship began doing the most amazing things you can imagine. One moment it would blend into the sunset, matching every color and pattern. Then it would go like oily water and abruptly change to a polished mirror or a dark, non-reflective surface like a hillside. It took long minutes for us to work our way to the clearing near the ship. It seemed like Mike was dragging me along while I wanted to move more cautiously, and to stop and look around more often. He was like that when we were hunting, always pushing ahead and flushing the game when I wanted to go slowly and work my way in for an easy shot.

We did not see any people near the ship as we walked up, and did not see the amazing silent ramp lower itself to the ground. However, we became aware that a man was standing next to one of the huge legs that supported the ship. The man made eye contact with us and had started to speak before we suddenly realized there were two of them. The one who had started to talk to us continued speaking, turning to the other as he spoke.

"These boys would like to touch our ship. Make sure it is well grounded, for we probably have developed some electricity in our travels." There was no greeting. I think he simply picked the top item off the jumbled pile of our thoughts and responded to it. He was speaking to us in that flawless German I remembered from before.

Then we were given the opportunity to touch something from another galaxy for the first time. The feeling of touching the ship, which definitely sent a chill up my spine, is also very difficult to explain. I expected it to be hard and metallic, but to this day, I find it hard to believe the feeling I had touching something that was so smooth and exchanged no heat with my hand. It was neither warm nor cold, and was definitely smoother than glass or polished metal, which will stick to your hand. It was like trying to press one magnet against the same pole of another, like I was not really touching anything at all. I think I was getting very close to it, but not actually touching it. The colors were somehow projected from inside it, or emanated from it, instead of reflecting as from a painted surface or a mirror. At that particular moment, the colors seemed to match the sky and even the clouds.

Mike put both his palms flat against it and then pressed his ear and cheek against it, but didn't say a thing. His expression told me that he was as perplexed about it as was I. The thought came to me that maybe the colors came from the other side and were just passed through the ship so we could see them on this side.

I still cannot explain it to my own satisfaction today. The ship was made in such a way, or of such a material, that once it rose several hundred feet in the air, it looked just like the sky. The reflection was the same as air, not like metal or a mirror. You just could not see the spaceship and there was no clue to help you pick it out from the background of the sky. Even standing there and touching that ship, it was hard to believe it was really there. We had realized another of our goals, but it had only created dozens of new questions, many more than it answered.

I remembered the times we watched the ship departing from the valley, how it rose in the air and then disappeared. Had it flown off so quickly that we couldn't follow its movements, or had they just floated there and watched our behavior? Had they been there watching us on those many trips to the valley when we saw nothing? Were those odd feelings I could recall when we moved through the "empty" valley actually the sensation of them watching us?

We accomplished our next goal in short order when we found ourselves shaking the hand of one of the visitors. It was his actual hand, not through a glove like I had often seen them wear. It was like shaking hands with the priest. The hand was soft and warm, the grip firm. Although I was right in the middle of what was probably the biggest thrill I ever had, I found myself thinking. "Sure would like to get into that ship." I began to wonder how to hint and ask if they would let us into their ship.

"I think that can be arranged," was the man's reply to the unspoken question, "but first," he added, "you will have to go through a 'process' to enter the ship. There is nothing to be afraid of. Nothing will harm you." He also stated, in such a way as not scare us, "You will have to go through the process again to leave the ship." I thought it was germs they were concerned about. We did not know much about it, but were confident that they certainly did.

He said this process was controlled by what I imagine we might call today a laser, or maybe an invisible energy beam or field of radiation. He went on to reassure us again that it would not hurt us, and compared it to the energy field that would not let you approach the ship. I understood that it was a modified form of the invisible shield. I was dismayed that the subject of entering the spaceship seemed to have passed on with no action.

While we were standing there beneath the ship, waiting to enter, he was explaining to us why the gophers and rabbits would run up to the shield and just kind of bounce back and run away. They were facing the same problems with the magnetic force that we were. We had quite a discussion with him on this subject while we waiting for them to let us inside. Our escort said, "You will soon begin to see things that will be coming to you in the next thirty years." I wasn't sure what he meant, but was just anxious to go inside.

His companion looked on as he was trying to explain these things to us, those ancient eyes seeing every detail of what was happening. I finally began to recognize that they were giving us information in some way other than by just what they told us. While we stood close to them, we could feel the warmth they all had toward us. It was growing stronger all the time. I began to understand they were communicating with us, not so much by what they were saying and we were hearing, but more by what we were feeling and what was going on inside us when they spoke.

We felt very relaxed around this man and his silent companion. They seemed to have something about them that other people we had met before did not have. When I look back, I think that perhaps it is the other way around. Maybe they lacked something that was present in everybody we had met before. I am certain that hatred and violence are not a part of their behavior; it does not seem to exist with them. Although there was only one of them speaking directly with us, I had the impression they were all nearby and listening closely to our conversation.

These people seemed to believe us when we talked to them. We talked about the droughts and the other real things in our life. They were very good listeners and were able to get us to talking about anything and everything. Whatever the topic, they seemed to understand. It was totally different from our first meeting, where we were tongue-tied and they did most of the talking. They seemed to realize that our world was in trouble, and understood about the depression and the drought as we talked about failed crops and the grasshoppers that were invading our country. They seemed to understand fully, and gave us the impression that the people of our planet had somehow brought these troubles on themselves and would have to solve these problems through their own efforts. They gave us the indication that man would soon bring terrible wars and suffering upon himself. It was mighty grim stuff for a couple of farm kids hoping for a look inside a spaceship.

As the years since then have gone by, everything they told us has happened, though sometime with strange and unexpected twists. How they knew these things in advance, I do not know. According to them, man has his own mind and he will use it to create and solve his own problems; he will advance until he hits a certain point in his growth, and then he will face a barrier or an interference that will develop from that one critical point, and he will eventually get himself into a lot of trouble.

If I understood them correctly, man must be free from outside control to survive here on the Earth. If this freedom is ever taken away from him, he will get confused and will revolt. Since that time, I have seen that leaders can push men only so far toward creating and building new things. In this modern world, we are in danger of losing our ability to think for ourselves. All these things were communicated to us, but they were so far ahead of our youthful lives at that time, it was impossible for us to grasp the full meaning of what they were telling us.

Their strange method of communication without words as well as the sensation of speaking with all of them while talking to any one of them makes it difficult to pin down exactly when we talked about a particular topic. Sometimes the meaning of their words did not come to me until days, weeks, or even years later. Then, I would see or hear something that made their words come ringing back to me through time. It became difficult to separate my own thoughts from theirs. Mike was all eyes and ears and let me do most of the talking, though they often made comments to him that would make him grin and wiggle, just like a little puppy dog.

In our conversations with them, they mentioned the taxes that have become such a burden to us all in present times. Back then, in the years before income taxes existed, I imagined that taxes were something like the war reparations that Germany was refusing to pay. They said that people would start resisting their own governments and eventually destroy the roots of their society. Then they said the governments would try to create new societies that the people cannot cope with. You can imagine the impression this talk had on two kids like us. I didn't even know what "society" was. I could see Mike was trying to be polite, but was wished he could get something going or make an excuse to leave. He was acting like he usually did at church.

According to them, the white people and the black people would eventually have an all-out difference that would result in war between them. This tension between the races would begin to build in my lifetime. We had seen black people several times before in railroad stations, and heard there were many of them "down South." Blacks, we knew, were "in for it," but in a different way than German Catholics.

We were also told that something called "corruption" in our government was at the heart of our problems. They said that if this "corruption" was controlled, and if our leaders faced the problems, they would save a lot of bloodshed. I tried to understand what government corruption might be, and came up with a picture of gangsters who killed all the cattle and then buried them while the people went hungry. Listening to them then, I felt the first twinges of disappointment creeping into the excitement of the moment. They were beginning to sound like Mr. Brooks and our parents, with all their talk of death and money. The grim realities of adult life were pressing in on our young minds. I could only hope then, as I do now, that the leaders of all nations allow their citizens the freedom to do their own thinking.

I certainly hope that our leaders will remember our need to be free, even as they begin to accept the fact that people from another galaxy are often visiting us. It is my hope that these visitors will always be friendly. They cannot come to Earth to straighten up our problems, though every time they come here they meant to help us. Let us have hope that they will always be so pleasant. I am sure, in many ways, they have left us knowledge. Maybe they have even left us the knowledge to solve our problems. They have mysterious ways for the human mind to understand.

A jab in the ribs brought me back from the dreamlike state in which I listened to the words of our guide, back from the adult world of war, taxes, politics, and corruption. My brother Mike was whispering to me, "This is taking an awful long time, Leo. I want to get into this ship in the worst way. Now I don't know if they will let us in or just lecture us all night long."

Deep down we were both crawling with curiosity, and feeling they were reading our minds. That was one thing that Mike and I definitely agreed upon in our earlier discussions about them. They always knew how we felt and the questions we wanted to ask even before we could open our mouths. We felt they were taking impulses from us which told them exactly what we thought and wanted to do. I decided if that was the way they worked, I would go along with them. I was reciting over and over in my head: "Go in the ship!" and was picturing Mike and me walking up that ramp and through the opening in the side of the ship. I know Mike was doing about the same thing. He kept glancing up at the ship above us and then over at the man we who was lecturing us. He had that kind of look he always got on his face when he wanted Mom or Dad to buy him candy at the store.

We kept on listening to them until, finally, we were invited with their particular kind of deep sincerity, to go into the spaceship. But they again told us we would have to have an adjustment—we would have to go through a procedure to go into this spaceship and a similar procedure to leave.

The huge ramp descended silently, seeming to sprout from the darkening sky. Almost before we knew it, we were escorted up the ramp by the man we had been speaking directly with and at last found ourselves entering the ship. There was an inner door and an outer door. When one door opened, the other door closed. Some kind of mist would go across the door. We asked him what it was. He told us that the mist was a "disinfectant," as we would call it.

"This will kill any germs on our bodies," he told us. "The area we are in is also disinfected." There we were in the space between the two magical doors. They were magical to me because, even up close, I could not tell how they opened and closed. One moment there was a wall, the next it was an open door. I could see no hinges or handle, not even a joint where the door met the smooth surface of the wall. The light inside interested me as well. Although we mostly used kerosene lamps at home, I had seen electric light bulbs and knew what brilliant, glaring light they produced. I wanted to see if the men from space were still using kerosene for lights, and if they did have electricity, what their light bulbs looked like. Well, you can imagine how disappointed I was to find out that they didn't have any light bulbs at all!

After we entered the compartment and the door had closed behind us, our guide told us we had to remove our clothes so the disinfecting process would be effective. Mike and I were both a little nervous about taking off our clothes in front of these people, but felt a little better about it when we saw that we would get to wear some of their clothing. I was glad we had both taken baths the night before. I was looking around for light bulbs or fixtures or switches, but there was nothing on the walls or the ceiling. There weren't any shadows, either. The light just seemed to come from everywhere at once. After we had dressed in their clothing, which opened at the back like one of those hospital gowns, we passed into another compartment which contained some kind of haze that went over our entire bodies.

They had given us some light jackets to put on that, compared to any clothing we had ever seen, were just beautiful. They were made from material of a very slick texture. I had never seen this kind of fabric before. The man who was with us watched as Mike put his arms into the sleeves with the opening in front, and then he said, "It will work that way, but it will fit better this way." He slipped it off and then back on with the opening to the back. Mike was kind of short then and the edge of the jacket almost brushed the floor. When the edges of the fabric were brought together, they attached themselves without buttons. I was glad I got to watch Mike put his on first, because then I put mine on right the first time, just like I had done it that way every morning since I was born.

When the inner door eventually slid open, we came into what must have been their main compartment. The first thing I noticed was their chairs. They were wonderful, just out of this world—never before have I seen anything at all like them. Our host invited us to sit in these great chairs. These chairs were completely adjustable, though the travelers were all so similar to each other, I am certain one size of chair would fit them all. It is hard for me to explain their construction clearly, for they were built quite differently from anything I had ever seen and, like the ship itself, didn't seem to have any individual parts. A force of some kind made them move toward you when you were about to sit without anyone appearing to touch them. How could a chair know when you want to sit? I thought maybe it was just our hosts being polite and somehow moving the chairs for us. As soon as he figured out how they worked, Mike had a great time trying to outwit the chairs, to the great amusement of our friendly hosts. When I sat, the chair subtly and automatically adjusted to fit and support my body from my heels to my head.

Looking up from my comfortable seat, I noticed what I thought then was a small movie screen. I suppose today we would call it a TV set or a computer monitor. You can just imagine how I felt, my excitement at the thrilling experience I faced. The size of the screen was about four feet by five feet. It was showing pictures of a place or process we could not fathom. I could not understand what we were seeing. The things that we saw on that screen are still in my mind, but I cannot explain what they meant—probably never will be able to. Along the wall opposite the screen was another type of machine which seemed to be operating continuously. I would assume, at the present time, we would describe them as computers, although they explained that these machines were a "magnetic sensor." All this, remember, took place back in the year 1932.

Their meals and the cooking are impossible to explain, although they were very nice about trying to explain it to us. We saw what I would call sleeping compartments with unusual beds, but we asked no questions about their sleeping customs. The toilet facilities were fully automatic, things like towels and toilet tissue were not there. It all seemed to be operating by the "magnetic" force, or maybe some chemical reaction. Even today I cannot explain it because it is something that existed in another world. We did not have enough knowledge to absorb all those things as children. I probably wouldn't do much better seeing it all for the first time as an adult.

The largest room we saw was their laboratory or workshop. Upon entering my eyes widen. I saw many different things I could not even begin to grasp. So many different things were happening there that I could not understand. I tried to ask some questions about these machines.

They replied to us, "No matter how we explain it to you, it would be impossible for you to understand any of it."

"Why do you keep coming to our valley?" Mike piped up.

"We study the life patterns," was the answer.

They more or less dropped the subject on that. However, I did notice one other thing that seemed to conflict with our earlier observations of the ship. We could not see into the ship from the outside. There was no transparent glass or window. However, from the inside in the upper part of the ship, we could see clearly through to the outside and observe clouds in the darkening sky. I realized you could see out through at least part of the side of the ship, but not in. We called it glass, but they informed us it was some other type of material which they did not explain more clearly to us.

Our host was pointing out what I thought was an excellent photograph of a sunset on the wall that focused from a camera high in the air. The picture showed a tremendous area of what I recognized as the Killdeer Mountains as they might look from a high hill in the area. Then I noticed that the tiny lights on the highway were moving, as were the clouds. It was a moving picture that seemed to be running all the time. It was evidently information that was being fed in from their sensor systems. I assume the sensor system transmitted the view to their TV screen. The two men who were working around the machines moved smoothly and efficiently and never got the least bit excited. They would glance at the picture view on the wall from time to time like they already knew what was going to happen.

There was no indication they were worried about being discovered or even had the slightest thought of destroying anything. Every indication their movements and behavior gave us was that they were very busy with many tasks and were strictly on a peaceful mission. I got the clear impression that the only way we could ever have any problems with these people was by directly interfering with their work or by trying to destroy them. Naturally, I think their ship would just swoop away from persons who meant them harm. No doubt, under the circumstances, they could use their magnetic lasers to hold attackers at a distance or to repel bullets or bombs. I can assure you, I believe these lasers could be very destructive if they wanted to use them as weapons. They could use their lasers in so many different ways, as they demonstrated to us. Maybe they could use the same type of machine to defend themselves.

That first visit inside their ship could have lasted only a few hours, but while we were there, it seemed to last for days. I believe that part of the reason for this is their advanced form of communication. While they are speaking to you about one thing, at the same time they can fill your mind with thoughts and information about many other things that you hardly even notice. Maybe this is what happens when you speak to someone who is tremendously intelligent. It was the same every time we were near them, even just watching them near the ship from our perch on the hillside. The ideas they gave us came trickling back out of our brains later on and often could not be told from our own.

Another of their abilities that we experienced inside that spaceship is just as baffling. I sat in one of those wonderful chairs watching the sun go down over the mountains outside and listening to one of our hosts trying to explain something about how far away their galaxy is. I was wondering if a galaxy is the same as a planet, or more like a star, and if it gets as much snow as we do in the winter, and if they have streetlights like Bismarck. Next thing I knew we are walking on the hillside and he was showing us how the grasshoppers lay their eggs under the dirt. Just like that. I blinked my eyes and there we were, back with the galaxy lecture. Blink again and he was showing us how the magnetic laser beam worked.

They could stop a bird in flight and hold it motionless in midair. Now I saw this done, but I am not sure how. I guess they just automated it. As my brother said to me, "You have to see this to believe it." They could catch a rabbit in his jump and stop him in midair, just make him stand still. They could hold these animals like this for minutes or hours. Then, suddenly, they could just release them and they went on their way like nothing had happened. The bird was free and so was the rabbit. In other words, from the understanding we gained, they had the ability to stop any moving object at any range they desired. Our military men should take note. They could reverse the trajectory or path of a moving object at any time, and could return anything that was thrown at them, right back to the spot from where it came.

After learning all these things, we just knew, in no way was anyone on Earth going to hurt our friends. We knew there was no way they would possibly think of hurting anyone on Earth, because they were in a position to stop all movement around them. In this way, they could take away the opportunity for any problems to arise.

We were told that they will continue traveling to our planet, to this very spot, and to many other places as our world gets deeper into trouble. Mike and I considered them highly intelligent beings. Everything they did was done perfectly—there were no errors. If anyone should ever get close enough to these men, I am sure he would admit, by just looking at them, that they are just peaceful and have no intentions of harming anyone. One of the reasons for their great intelligence is their ability to use twelve senses. They told us that twelve people from their galaxy live full time on our planet Earth. These people live among us but we cannot tell that they are different from us. We were also informed that these twelve people have often offered to help our world and were rejected every time. No one was interested in talking with them. These people from another world must be asked and must be made welcome before they will give advice.

Can you imagine that we have had the opportunity to work with and learn from these people who have the knowledge of all twelve senses, and we have rejected it? I felt that if we see someone who seems to be beyond us, we should listen to them. We do not have to take their advice, but we should at least consider it.

Colleges and universities should welcome these people, so that our scholars can form an opinion of the value their teachings might have for us. Our scientists also should open their minds toward these goals. I believe scientists today have finally realized there are unusual movements between galaxies, and possibly have enough knowledge to understand that there is interplanetary traveling going on. These people who we met and talked to back in the year 1932 came right out and told us they had traveled to this planet for over five thousand years. They will continue coming to this planet because it is their responsibility. It is important for us to understand that they said the *Earth* is their responsibility, rather than mankind. We only occupy a place they are trying to take care of.

This all proves one thing to me—that they certainly do have a longer life than we have. They must take care of their health much better than the people here on Earth. In a roundabout way, they told us that. They told us so much, yet people will not believe us. People on Earth must come to their senses and understand that these advanced people we have met do exist, and that they are connected with an advanced civilization or supreme being that somehow exists beyond the twelve galaxies. I do not know why the number twelve figured into so many of the things they explained to us. All I can do is relate knowledge I sometimes do not fully understand, because it was delivered to us by visitors from another galaxy.

I believe that many stories we have read about contacts with visitors from space are misunderstood, improperly explained, or outright false. Those of us who have experienced the visitors must examine our minds and tell the true story of what happened. Those who are not truthful will have to take the consequences for untrue things they say about these highly intelligent beings. We ourselves do not want people to spread falsehoods about us. I learned more in a short period from these people than I could have by years of study anywhere else on Earth. I am sure that, in some way, they have been spreading knowledge among us throughout history. We have just not accepted it, or have claimed it as our own. We, the people, are going to have to work toward recognizing and understanding the information they are providing us. These people, I feel, are not doing this directly through books and television. They are doing it through some kind of brain wave transmission that produces effects in us all, similar to what Mike and I experienced, though at a much lower level. For our own survival, we must admit they are far ahead of us and poses important information that is vital for us to learn. We are dealing with people who share thoughts and information with each other, and with us, all the time. If we could live more like them, we would have much less friction and trouble in this world. There are better worlds beyond this that are just waiting for us.

We must accept the fact that they are among us, are powerful beyond our imaginations, and are responsible for protecting our planet. The people of Earth are going to have to accept these facts and live with one another in peace instead of fighting with each other to the detriment of the planet.

We are going to have to forget our pride and learn to live with it. If we do not accept their knowledge, we will surely destroy ourselves. They said that if we eliminate things that are harmful to our bodies, we can increase our life span up to two hundred and fifty or three hundred years. Some scientists today would agree on this. It is just a matter of learning enough to get started. This knowledge is available to us from these visitors to our Earth if we will only ask for it.

There is no way they can be identified or traced, no matter how many agencies or organizations may try, or how many tests or examinations might be attempted. Just think about it. Remember—we are dealing with beings who can penetrate our brains. Whenever someone can penetrate our thoughts, there is no way we can detect them. They can make us see or think anything they want, just like a hypnotist. They are undetectable and indestructible people who are kind and benevolent toward us. But in our thinking about them, we must consider that they will not let us cross their border lines. If we do not begin to help them in their responsibility to care for the Earth and begin to do something about the problems that are affecting our planet, we may develop some problems with them.

Man has always wondered and dreamed about travel into outer space. Man has now succeeded in traveling into space and has walked on the moon. Why do we feel that people from another galaxy cannot travel to our planet? Is it our pride? Are we unable to accept the fact that we really are not number one? When I was a child and these things were actually happening to me, I was not thinking like this. The years that have passed since then have allowed these thoughts and beliefs to come to me.

The time is here for people on Earth to review their minds and not feel that we are the only people to travel in the universe. I have not been trying to keep to myself the knowledge I received back in 1932 from these people from another galaxy. I have repeatedly tried to tell others about these things and have been mocked and ignored. The things they told us have taken place. It is important that we should try to contact one of these people who are living with us on Earth. We would be certain to learn from him. This, I am sure, is not going to be easy to do unless we are very sincere and show no greed. As I understand them, they do not exist with all these negative and useless thoughts.

For years we have not respected these flying spaceships. They have been called them falling stars, flying saucers, and swamp gas, and we have considered them to be imaginary. I believe the time has come to admit they are here and begin to show respect for them. There is nothing to fear and we can only gain. Although we have started doing some things for ourselves, we are not doing enough and are just poking along at it. If we discipline our own minds, we will become more useful to our world. We must respect other people for what they are and not give up hope that we can improve our lives by improving our world. In the same peaceful way that the visitors work, we can guide others into useful behavior without military threats, laws, and restrictions.

Forty-three years ago is when my experiences with these people first started. Through the years, I found that almost everything people were doing seemed to be backwards from the knowledge I gained from the visitors. I learned that ours is one of twelve galaxies that are, in some way, tied together. How or why these galaxies are related, how ours became one of the twelve, which galaxy we are in, we did not ask them. I had a million questions, but this is something that will have to be figured out by some astronomers or scientists.

We tried to understand and I have tried to put the pieces together over the years. I came up with the idea that knowledge and intelligence are definitely in all twelve galaxies. It is this knowledge that is coming to us from another world. These people who are traveling to and from our planet have some very strong connections with our survival.

* * * * * *

These are my views and beliefs. I have put them down to the best of my knowledge and according to the understanding I have received from these intelligent beings who are continuously traveling to our Earth. Over the years, I have spent approximately eight and one-half hours talking and visiting with these people, most of it back in 1932. Though I was not very old at the time, the memories remain clear and distinct. The human mind does not forget things like that. My experiences have only strengthened my belief that there definitely is a supreme being or intelligence that has a close connection with the visitors. It is these people and this intelligence who are the source of much that our world has experienced and will continue to experience in the future.

Because this information was received and understood in such a roundabout way, it is difficult to explain and to understand. It is impossible to prove in terms that would be acceptable to a scientist or to a court of law. I can only hope that in some way our scientists and leaders in all the world's nations will make a sincere effort to waste less time and money planning how to fight and win wars. We must learn to use our money and our resources in more productive ways.

Our leaders have wasted time, money, and lives on warfare throughout history. Man has often felt he has won or gained by a war. But if we think honestly and consider all the costs, deep down we must admit to ourselves that we have always lost more than we have gained. We must begin to admit that we have never really gained anything through violence and hostility. The intentions of many of our leaders were good, but things never seem to come out in the end the way they were intended. Have you ever really considered what we might have done for the people on Earth if all our nations had taken the energy we have devoted to war and put it to productive use? I am certain we could have eliminated a tremendous amount of suffering and could have extended our individual life spans by many years. Perhaps we would not have population problems on our hands as we do today. Perhaps we, too, would be traveling from one galaxy to the next.

It is never too late to change. It is never too late to direct our educational system toward goals for the greater benefit of our people and the protection of our home planet. I know these intelligent human beings have traveled to our planet for several thousands of years to fulfill a responsibility they owe to something that is beyond even them. Let us not put them in the position of having to clean up our mess. Let's clean up our own mess. If we can walk on the moon, we can certainly do this. Let us put back into the Earth what we have taken from it. Over the years, we have taken so much and have returned so little. We cannot continue taking forever with no thought for the future, for eventually there will be nothing left to take.

I know we think we are doing a good job, but we really are not. We must remember that we have on this planet Earth twelve people who come from another galaxy. This was clearly explained to us. They are willing to work with us if we will only ask for their help. We must remember that they are highly intelligent and may only give us hints as to what we should do for ourselves. They will not take control of our lives or our world. I feel we should take full advantage of anything they can do to help us deal with our problems. Each of us must examine our mind and convince ourselves they do exist, and that we are not going to fight them in any way. We must show good faith and peaceful efforts toward them. I feel they are more than willing to give us knowledge that we need to succeed at improving our world because it will make their task easier. Also, we must accept that we will have to somehow make up for all the wrongs we have done to our world. Remember that they can penetrate our minds and will know instantly if we are sincere or not. Consider this in your own life. None of us is too small or too unimportant to take the first step. Remember how much time and effort they spent talking with two farm boys in the hills of North Dakota.

From my experience, I am certain they communicate with one another without speaking. Their thoughts must be organized and peaceful, for they always were very contented and looked very happy. We must accept that this form of communication does exist. We can eliminate our hatred and greed and do something for ourselves, because that is the only way we are going to get any help from them. These beings from another galaxy will not push themselves on us. If we just ask them, they will help us. If we do not ask them, then we cannot expect help from them.

They do not visit us to take over and control our lives in any way. This was made clear to us. When we do ask for answers, we must have good intentions. We must not hope to use their help for personal gain. Our good intentions can benefit all human beings on this Earth. Always remember that these people from another galaxy are capable of penetrating our minds. We cannot lie to them, for if we do, we will not gain anything. They will just ignore us.

If our leaders on this planet feel they could somehow capture one of these men today, what do you think would happen? They would probably want to lock him up and question him to get information about building and flying those amazing ships or creating the invisible barrier. But just think for a moment. How can you imprison someone who can read your mind and literally make you see, hear, and feel anything he wants? You would be unable to tell if you had them or not. You could not conceal your intention to capture one of them. How could you lay the trap? They could tell you everything they know and then cause you to forget it the moment you walk away from them.

From my experience in 1932, I found that, although they did not question us, they had no problem in getting us to talk about our lives. Why were they interested in our lives? They gave us a lot of good, secure feelings and left us free to come and go as we pleased. They were always very nice and mannerly toward us, like we were real grown-up human beings, and always attempted to answer our questions. Also, they would sometimes make themselves very clear on certain subjects. But it was impossible for us to understand the reasoning behind their efforts. I think this is something we can learn to do among ourselves. The day is gone when we say it was just a falling star or some gas that has formed in a swamp and looks like a flying object. We have to admit that we have some beings among us from another galaxy. They are human, just like us, only they have developed far beyond us. Just how far ahead of our own level of civilization they are, I do not know, but I am certain our intelligence is very low compared to theirs. We must learn to express our positive feelings toward them. They are here to help us on their own terms. We must let them know that we more than welcome their help.

From my experience, I would say they are free and at peace. Perhaps these are skills or abilities we can and should learn, for the world seems to be seeking freedom and peace. No one seems to understand that our methods of achieving these goals are not working and are definitely going to have to change. Money and power will have to become part of the past. These are things we will have to realize. If we are able to understand this, we will then be able to decide what will happen to our world, not the caretakers from another galaxy. As they put it to us—before we can help you, you must first help yourselves.

Throughout our history, we have not learned to do this. We have only worked ever harder to figure out a way to beat someone, to make an extra dollar the others cannot make, or to create a hardship for our competition. A tremendous amount of hardship has been created in just that way.

I have always believed that peace and freedom are goals we should be working for. I feel that is why I had the experience of meeting these people from another galaxy. No matter how many people I could talk to, whether it was five hundred or five thousand, I could not receive the amount of knowledge and feeling that I received from them in only a few hours.

Again, it is hard to explain why I have these feelings about them. They just gave me the feeling I could trust them and that I could confide in them. All they seemed to have toward me was trust. That made me feel very welcome.

When the time came for us to leave them and return to the farm, our minds were full and tired and the evening had grown quite late. Again, we had learned all we could at one time, and they seemed to agree with us. As we were preparing to leave, they assured us they would see us again in the future. It was our last contact with them that year.

The years following our first contact with the visitors, our mother died after giving birth to my sister, Mary. We also got electricity just about that time. Dad had his hands full trying to take care of me, Mike, and our little brother Hank. Now there was Mary. We had to send her to live with my aunt for the first three years of her life, though she got to come home and stay with us over the summers. We all went to visit her once a month while she was away from us and were all happy when she came back to live with us permanently. After that, the county nurse came out to visit us once a month and seemed to check everything in the house each time she was there. I guess we did okay, because we all managed to stick together. Before she died, Mother told me to be sure to take care of everyone because I would survive them all. When Mary grew old enough to go to school, Dad put her in a private school in New England, North Dakota, but she still came home to visit on the weekends until she graduated from high school. I even spent time in a private school and got enough education to see me through my life.

I saw the spaceship off and on after that first year, and even saw it land several times. In 1933, I had the pleasure of seeing it landing about two miles south, and a mile and a half east of Dunn Center, North Dakota. It continued landing at that location from 1933 to 1934. No one in Dunn Center seemed to mention it or pay any attention to it. Politics was the big topic of discussion then, with a lot of talk about whether or not we should pacify Hitler in Europe. Most of us thought President Herbert Hoover was a big part of our problems. He campaigned by promising two chickens in every pot. Franklin Roosevelt campaigned from the train in Killdeer around then, and said "I can't give you two chickens in every pot—I only promise one." During that period of time, I did not make any more personal contacts with the visitors. They never appeared during the winter, only during the spring or the hot summer weather.

In August of 1936, about the end of the month, around 9:45 in the evening, I again saw their ship land at the location near Dunn Center and decided to walk up to them. As I approached the ship, I was allowed to enter through their magnetic forces. The ship didn't look any different from the ship I'd seen four years ago in 1932.

I was welcomed by three people and was certain they were the same people I had met back in 1932.

Since they did not use individual names, it is hard to say for sure. When I found myself back with them, it was like they were old friends and I experienced no fear at all. I did not have to ask to enter their spaceship—they asked me to come in. Again, that same feeling came over me. I found them most welcoming—the feeling was very good, like going to visit my grandparents for Thanksgiving or Christmas.

We talked then about things of the future to a small degree. They said the world would have many problems, but they would not interfere in any way with our handling of these difficulties. In our conversation, they reaffirmed that this planet was their concern, that man has his own mind, and that he must learn to take care of his planet if he wants to keep his home. This man from the spaceship assured me our planet would continue to exist. But I was not assured that man would continue to exist on it, if he did not learn to take better care of his most valuable possession. One other strange thing they confirmed was what my mother said before she died, that I would be the last surviving member of the family. They said I would see the world in a lot of trouble before the year 2000.

There was no further contact with them until 1938, in the Watford City, North Dakota, area, close to the Missouri River Bridge. I was driving about two miles south, and a mile and a half west of the bridge near an opening in the hills. In this opening, I spotted a spaceship at rest on the ground. After pulling my car off the road, I got out and walked down to the area where the ship had landed. It was the same ship. As I neared the ship, I found myself quite free and was not kept away by that magnetic force.

By the year 1938, I had reached the age of eighteen. I knew I was not imagining the visitors anymore, but found I had made some true friends. These people were among the very few people I could relate with. I had often tried to talk to different people about the men from the spaceship, but again and again, nobody would understand or believe me. They were not interested in investigating or even offering to go with me. When my friends from the stars told me no one would believe me, they were so very right. In general, I have found that everything they told me has been true. They did not mislead me in any way. This honesty and directness, I felt, made them my true friends. I have cherished their friendship through the years, often thinking they were the only ones, next to Mike, who could understand the problems of my life. Each visit with them was like going home to a family that loved me.

In our discussions, they gave me the indication that the areas where they land were of concern to them, and are important in terms of what man is doing to the planet. As I said, they spoke very good English and German. In those early visits, they spoke mostly in German to us. Now they spoke to me in English, perhaps because I had grown more accustomed to speaking English since my childhood. I certainly did not imagine them to mean me harm in any way. Over time, I found I began to understand more clearly many of the things they had told us earlier. Every word they said to me, I believe was true, and gained more meaning for me as I was able to reflect upon the ideas over time.

I did not see them again until 1939, after I had been working at Sidney, Montana, for about three months. On September 15, about 9:30 P.M., I was on my way to Watford City, North Dakota, not even thinking of a spaceship at all. Suddenly, I spotted something moving across the sky in front of my car, about two thousand feet up in the air. I turned off on the first dirt road I came to, for something told me to do this. It was just a rough side road and I followed it maybe three and a half miles off the main road. Soon I saw that spaceship again. This time, it was at rest perhaps three hundred feet off the side road in a level clearing. I sat in my car and watched it for about five minutes, then decided to walk down to the ship.

There was no movement of any kind, but I felt free to approach the ship. It didn't seem to affect me in any way. When I was within one hundred feet of this huge spaceship, I noticed the unusual door opening, and two people coming out raising their hands toward me. As I moved forward, I hoped they were the same people I had met before. After I had approached within five feet of them, one of them walked up to me, put his hand on my shoulder and said, "It is good to see you again."

As we walked toward the spaceship, both of the other men came over and also individually put a hand on my shoulder and said, "It is good to see you again." My heart had jumped into my throat. They were my friends, the same men I had met before.

One of them also said to me, "We always look forward to seeing you—we feel you respect us deeply."

Mike and I had more than deep respect for them.

He looked at me and stated, "You have changed quite a bit since 1932."

I replied, "I have noticed no change in you at all. I don't quite understand this, but it does not really concern me."

"We are several thousand years ahead of your time," he answered. "We are germ free and our life expectancy is quite different from yours. At this time, it would be impossible for us to explain to you how we have accomplished all this in our lives. These things you would not understand. But we can assure you, if your scientists would devote their time to increasing your life span, people on Earth would be capable of living in good health much longer than you do now."

These were all the answers I received from them on this subject. This conversation took place outside the spaceship. The time was about ten o'clock at night, but for some reason, the area around the spaceship was not dark. Some type of glow kept shadowless light in the area. It was the same type of lighting I remembered from our previous visits with them.

I asked them, "Does this light show up for any great distance?"

They replied, "Yes."

I asked them if they were worried about people noticing it.

They replied, "You have been cleared to enter our area, and as you have noticed, there was no movement around you when you were coming over to our ship. We have stopped all movement for three miles around us. There is no way that anything can move within that area. No person can approach the ship unless we allow them entrance. It will be some time, well in the future, before people will be able to understand and do much if any of what we are capable of doing now. This new understanding will make a tremendous change on your planet Earth. Would you care to step into our spaceship with us again? There, we can fill you in on a few matters I believe will interest you. Remember, you will have to go through the same process as you did before. You understand this, don't you?"

"Yes," I replied. "I understand and I am not as scared as my brother and I were back then."

He smiled and said, "We will never forget those two frightened children that approached us back then. We knew you were there and tried to handle and treat you in such a way that the two of you would not be frightened. We knew your thoughts and understood your determination and your belief that we do exist. You must continue to always have faith in yourself, for faith and determination are your future."

After this brief conversation, we entered the spaceship. Upon entering the first compartment, I had to remove my clothes, and the mist covered my entire body. Another door opened and I was handed a jacket. Then I entered the main compartment. There were six men sitting in those miraculous chairs that I remembered so well from before. They appeared to be very relaxed, and were watching that big television screen, which had pictures on it I still could not understand. I asked them about it, and they answered me this way:

"The image comes from our galaxy, which is many millions of miles away. It is only meaningful to us in our work here. Do not waste your effort in trying to understand any of it."

I asked them how they lit the inside of their ship and the area nearby without light bulbs.

One of them replied, "Our lighting system is in our metal. The power for our machines is also generated in our metal. This is all we can tell you, for it would be impossible for you to understand how our energy system works. The ideas behind these systems are unknown to your scientists at this time. You have seen all these things with your own eyes, but you know by now that no one will believe any of it, no matter how you try to tell them."

By this time, it had grown quite late, maybe about 11:30 P.M. Finally, I said, "I think it is time for me to leave." It would take me some time, I told them, to make my way back. I would probably do quite a bit of stumbling before I got back to my car.

Then one of the men sitting in the chairs stood up and said, "We will take care of that problem."

The first man put his hand on my shoulder. After hesitating for a moment, I put my hand on his shoulder. In turn, I did this with all six men. After I entered the outer compartment, I removed the jacket and handed it inside to them. The door closed and again the mist covered my entire body. Quickly, I put my clothes back on, and as I finished dressing, the unusual door opened and I stepped back out of the spaceship. After a few moments hesitation at the top of the ramp while I savored the touch of the ship, I descended to the ground and started back for my car. In some mysterious way, they produced that amazing shadowless light all the way to my car. After I opened the door, got in, and started the engine, I looked over toward the spaceship. There was total darkness in that direction. It was as if they did not exist at all. I turned my car around and was on my way back to Watford City.

I had a very enjoyable visit with them, but I could not share it with anyone, because as they said, no one would believe it. All the way back to Watford City, I pondered why no one would believe me. Out of thirty or forty people whom I had talked to about this, none of them would take me seriously. I had made up my mind that people just were not interested. They simply did not care to learn anything about the future that would be coming to them. Could it be true that they did not care how their future might be changed as a result of knowledge given to the world by these human beings from another galaxy? There were times I would have given anything if I could have found someone to go with me to witness my experiences. Maybe these people from another galaxy had something to do with that. They assured me I would be seeing them again in the future.

I lost contact with them in 1941, when I was called into the service of my country with the Navy. Most of my Navy career was spent in the South Pacific, where I served on board *Am 303 Amphibious Unit Minesweeper*. I participated in the invasions of Okinawa and Iwo Jima, and was in the occupation force in Japan. I had quite an experience with the kamikaze suicide planes on board the U.S.S. *Missouri*. Mike was younger than I by five years, but enlisted as soon as he was old enough and served in the Army during the last two years of the war. Mike served with Patton in the South Pacific where he earned two Purple Hearts and citations. He was transferred to Japan for the occupation, where he rose in the ranks and at one time handled the payroll for the entire occupation force in Japan. Mike decided that military life was for him and made the Army his career. My youngest brother, Henry, also joined the Navy and served in the South Pacific during the last part of the war. We were within two hundred miles of each other but always seemed to miss each other in port and never managed to get together. He was discharged from the Navy with a disability after the war. Throughout our wartime experiences, neither Mike nor I saw anything of the visitors from space.

In the years immediately following the war, I had no contacts with them. But for some reason, all the time I was in the service they constantly entered my mind. I just could not forget my experience with them. They predicted that violent and inhumane conflict, which went far beyond anything I could have imagined in our conversations. It was certainly not the kind of activity I thought they would approve of. But I do not know what we could have done to avoid all that suffering and loss of life. I have always hoped they were sympathetic with our side in that war, and hoped our country was doing the right thing at that time. I did my part and was very grateful to return home alive and in one piece.

After my discharge from the Navy in 1948, I moved back home to Killdeer, to the same area where my experiences with them first began. Though I still thought about them frequently and watched for their ship in the evening hours, I was very busy trying to put my life together again. Although I occasionally spotted the ship about the area in the months after my return home, for some reason I did not make personal contact with them.

After leaving Killdeer, North Dakota, in late 1946, I moved to Bozeman, Montana, and began to work as a salesman. My work required many miles of travel by road through country that is mountainous and very different from the area around Killdeer. Very often, I found myself returning to home late in the evening hours. Finally, in 1950, I saw a ship in Montana along the highway between Norris and Sappington Junction. I spotted them landing in the upper hills several miles off the main road. Remembering what they told me years ago, that they were landing all over our country and that we would one day meet again, I began to plan my trips so as to pass through the area in the evening on my way home. I began to spot them more frequently in the evening around 8:15, flying through the area into the sunset. Because the ship was usually well back from the highway in very difficult terrain, I had no real chance to make a personal contact with them. Often, I thought to myself that this country must suit their purposes by allowing them to work in remote locations with little chance of interruption.

Mike had been transferred from duty in Japan to serve in the Korean Conflict. He was reported killed in action in July of 1950, after earning a Silver Star and some other citations for that war. Our whole family felt his loss very deeply. By now I had my own family to support and was keeping very busy.

It was in 1962, when I had my three young daughters and two of their friends with me, that I saw a ship moving through the evening skies relatively near to the highway. I thought that this might be the opportunity I had longed for over the years—a chance to show the ship to the girls, so that others could confirm my sighting. The girls were not very old, maybe about Mike's age when we saw the ship at Killdeer, but I felt this was an opportunity they might remember—seeing something from another world. It was difficult to pick my way over the dark mountain roads in my passenger car, but finally I drove my car within about two hundred feet of the spaceship. It was hovering about twenty feet off the ground, producing all the colors I had witnessed before.

I said to the five nervous young girls, "Watch up there, just above us."

The girls were just like a flock of small birds, communicating their nervous excitement from one to the others almost immediately. It was very hard to contain my disappointment when I saw they were all frightened by the ship. There was no way to convince them no one would hurt us. We watched the ship for only about half an hour. Several times, I flashed my headlights at them, certain they knew the girls were with me and were scared at seeing this unusual ship hovering in the air. The girls had never seen anything like this before, and I hope they will never forget the experience. I am sure they have talked about it many times since.

I was convinced this was the same spaceship I had seen back in 1932, and again in 1939, and had no doubt that the same people were aboard. It continued to be my dream that some day I would be able to share this experience with someone who would understand it all and who would feel it and believe it. One never knows, maybe the whole world might be able to experience it with me. I hope that someday, someone with me will have a clear mind and good intentions. Perhaps they too can meet these visitors and experience touching them and seeing the inside of a ship from another world. However, I realize they would have the same problems I have had all these years in trying to get somebody to believe me. They would experience the same frustration as I have felt all these years. Like me, they probably would feel sure within themselves and yet be unable to get anyone to accept that the visitors do indeed exist and are here for a good purpose. It is quite a thing that a person faces, being certain inside, yet unable to prove it. But I guess life has always been that way.

In 1963, at about 7:45 on a summer's evening, I was driving from Ennis, Montana, to Sappington Junction, again all by myself. I spotted a spaceship from my car window, landing in the foothills about six or seven miles off the main highway. It was headed west, setting itself down into the sunset, so I stopped my car and got out to watch. While I was standing there along the highway, leaning against the fender of the car and watching the movements of the ship, another car pulled up behind me and stopped. The other driver, a middle-aged man, got out first. As I started walking over toward him, a woman got out also.

"Am I just seeing things?" I asked them. "Would you look over toward those hills and tell me what you see?"

The lady replied immediately. "I told my husband there was something flying in the air over toward those hills. I am sure you are not imagining any of this because it's still flying over there now." She was very excited. "My gosh, look! That monstrous thing is coming straight down. It looks like it is going to fall between those hills."

In my mind, I felt this was my first real chance to have someone confirm the sighting with me. Anticipating his interest, I confronted her husband, and asked him to follow me. My idea was to drive as close as we could and then walk the remaining distance to the ship.

He looked at me with wide, alarmed eyes and said, "Do you think I am crazy? You think you can talk me into getting involved with that thing? It's none of my concern and I surely will not make it my concern. If you don't care what happens to you, I certainly care what might happen to me and my family."

They started moving back to their car. I followed him over to his car and asked him to give me his name and address, so I could write him a letter and let him know if something should develop. I told him that I was going to explore this sighting further.

"I'm not going to give you my name and address," he said. "I don't want to be involved in this in any way. I've seen only one thing like this before. It was in California, and it was only a few hundred feet from my car. I hoped and prayed I'd never see another one again. You are the only person I have told about this."

He started his car and as he pulled around my car, he hollered, "Good luck!" and drove off rapidly down the highway.

Very disgusted, I sat in my car and pondered why people are so scared of something that is of no harm to them. Maybe it is all the science fiction scare stories that are circulating through the bookshelves today. Many times I asked myself why people are not interested. After all, this is their life, their country, their world, and they have the responsibility of paying attention to what is happening. I just assume that people who see something like this, in their mind, tell themselves that, if they ignore it, it will just go away. But I can assure them that, as long as our world continues to exist, the visitors will never just go away. They will always be with us for as long as people live on the Earth. They will always remain in our minds whether we realize it or not. Mankind will eventually have to recognize that visitors are here with us and we will have to learn to live with it.

On October 21, 1963, at about 8:15 P.M., I was driving through the area again and decided I just had to make the effort to reach the spot where I saw that ship landing. Maybe I had grown lonely for them, for I felt they were friends of mine, and I longed for their company and that remembered warmth of their presence. Driving my car along the dark mountain roads as close as I could get would still leave me about three miles to walk. Switching my parking lights on so I could find my way back in the dark, I began to walk back in. It was quite dark by the time I approached the top of the ridge, beyond which I felt the landing site must be located. There was the ship, sitting there and looking just like I remembered it when Mike was standing by my side. Since it had been a long walk, I stopped on the top of the hill to rest for a while. As I regained my breath, I had the feeling the spaceship must have been there for about an hour before my arrival. I was not a bit scared about what I might encounter out on that dark hillside. It is tough to explain, but I felt real joy and anticipation about seeing that ship again.

After resting for about five minutes, I decided I would just have to work my way down the hillside to the ship. It looked to be about a mile down a rugged slope to where the ship was resting. When I was about halfway down, I noticed the area around the spaceship was lit up with the soft, indirect light I remembered so well. I could see about six people moving about on the ground. As I came closer, I saw two of them were moving my way. I was certain they were coming to greet me. Not being frightened but feeling very relaxed, I held out my hand to greet them. They had that same welcome smile on their faces I had seen before. They seemed to be pleased to see me again after such a long time.

When they approached, I started walking a little faster, for I was very anxious to get close to them. Walking up to me, one of the men put his hand on my shoulder. Without saying a word, I then put my hand on his shoulder. I could feel him pressing my shoulder with his fingers, giving me the feeling he was more than just happy to see me.

After a short silence, he said, "It has been many years since we last saw one another."

"Yes," I replied with a big grin on my face. "It has been quite a while."

"You had quite an experience with those people out there on the highway," he said. "We monitored you on our sensor system. We could not help but listen to your conversation and thought you were doing a good job trying to convince the man to come along with you. Had he come with you, it would have showed that he was concerned about things to come, that he was willing to witness the sighting of our ship. You should have known, after all these years, that most people will not believe you. But this time was different. This man knew of our existence. He had seen us before. Instead of believing in us, he allowed his fear to convince him that we are a threat. He prefers to think that we do not exist. He has closed his mind to everything. Why people continue to fear us, we do not know. Throughout the years we have walked on this planet without harming anyone. Always, we have been willing to help, but no one seems to want our help. Let us walk down to the ship. You will certainly feel more relaxed with yourself there."

As we approached the ship, the other five men came out and greeted me with that same welcome smile on their faces. Placing our hands on one another's shoulders, we made their customary greeting. They all seemed to make this statement together: "It is the most welcome sight to see you again. We regret that your brother cannot be here with us. We enjoyed him very much." After I explained to them how Mike had been lost in Korea, I felt that they already knew what I was telling them. Perhaps more about it than I knew myself, but I did not push the question further. Following the same procedure, I entered the ship once more.

As we sat in the chairs, I experienced a brief image of Mike trying to outwit the chairs and plunk himself down before one could slip under his behind. When I looked at them, I saw that they were all smiling at the memory. It was very relaxed and casual as I talked with them about my experiences through the years since our last meeting. They mentioned my attempt to show the ship to my daughters, and regretted that the girls had been too frightened to see more. Then one of them began to tell me how man on Earth, in the last three years, had tried to learn how to detect and capture one of their ships.

He said, "There have been some determined attempts made to capture our ship. We always hope that man will change his mind and devote his energy for his own benefit. He has the ability to accomplish much good for himself, for the people of the world. Your science and technology have advanced enough to pose a threat to our ships, as well as to the entire planet." A picture of the mushroom cloud following an atomic blast filled my mind.

"If your military leaders continue their efforts to damage our ships, we will be forced to defend ourselves. Although we have been seriously provoked, we will not treat man like he treats us, making unprovoked attacks which threaten our lives. Our actions to protect and defend ourselves are governed by a simple principle: Anything that is thrown at us, will be thrown back to its source. We are telling you this because, if it should ever happen, and I believe that one day it will, we want you to know we will do no more than protect ourselves. Our laws allow us only the right to return anything that is thrown at us. We are allowed to return it to the same place it came from, back to the source."

We just sat there visiting and talking like old friends. Other than the issue of self-defense, we talked about things in general. There was no tour of the vessel, because I already knew what was there to see. I received the impression there was only one spaceship traveling about our planet at that time. They were concerned that people of the Earth were digging themselves ever deeper into trouble, and were creating problems they might one day not be able to solve. They gave me the feeling they were growing more concerned and were not at all happy with the state of our world.

After we left the ship, we sat on the ground for a while, all seven of us, looking up at the stars. We sat there talking about different things for perhaps another two hours. In my mind I thought of leaving and starting back for home. They could read my mind, so they knew what I was thinking.

"I must be leaving for home," I said.

One of them replied, "I hope we will see you again. It will be quite a while, though, because we are traveling back to our own galaxy. There will be another one of our spaceships traveling about your world, but they will make far fewer landings than we have. They will be more interested in what man is doing in outer space. We will have another, far larger ship, which will be landing in this same location on Earth in 1971, 1972, and 1973. You may have the opportunity to see this large ship in this area quite often."

Again, they reminded me to always believe and work to understand what I have experienced and seen, and not to forget that they are always willing to help if people would ask, and not fear them. With this understanding,

I told them I would always be concerned about their activities and would take every opportunity to see them again. I told them that they would always be the only true friends I have ever known.

We separated then with very deep feelings, and I started back for my car. Light was provided for me all the way back. I was about half a mile from the ship when I began to notice how warm the area around me seemed to be, although it had grown quite cold out. As I approached my car, I heard the motor running. I never understood how or why they had started my car. It was nice and warm as I climbed into it. How they could have done this, I do not know. Closing the door and shifting the car into gear, I turned around and headed back for the highway; when I finally reached the pavement, I stopped, got out of my car, and looked back for any lights, or other sign of the ship.

The mountains were dark and silent.

You can well imagine that I have devoted many hours of thought and reflection to these visitors from the stars. My attempt to write down a clear account of what I saw and experienced has been difficult in many ways that I did not expect. But I can now appreciate their efforts to answer our questions in ways a small boy could understand. They communicated most of their thoughts to us without using speech or words, which makes the task of explaining what I learned from them ever so much more difficult. We have no words in English, German, or any other language I know to speak or write about the many things, events and processes that are as common to them as washing our hands is to us. How do you explain to a bright kindergarten student the meaning of the information displayed on the screen of a computerized automobile engine analyzer, a gas chromatograph, or a CAT scan system? How do you explain how such a machine works or why it is important to your work?

I think it is as important to concentrate on the feelings and emotions they gave us as it is to try to understand their precise thoughts or learn their knowledge. Children and adults alike avoid things that frighten or repel them, or suggest that something might be dangerous or unwholesome in some way. Nothing about them gave us any hint of evil or trickery. They were wise, kind, and clean and never made us feel like stupid kids, as so many adults do without thinking. Their actions and behavior were always calm and considerate. I cannot imagine one of them making a mistake in anything. They are perfect role models, the kind of people each of us would like to be when we grow up. That is one of their most important messages: Mankind must grow up and mature to be entitled to poses their knowledge and abilities. I know they are very concerned about our nuclear and chemical weapons and our warlike nature. What a problem we must be for them, always threatening the health and safety of this beautiful planet, which is their responsibility to protect. The picture that comes to my mind is a crowd of unruly children fighting and playing in a carefully tended garden with no regard for the problems they are causing for the gardener.

The implications of what I have called their magnetic beam or shield, which must relate to the force that drives their ship between the galaxies, are enormous and far beyond our own understanding of physics. Their ability to return projectiles, such as bullets or rockets, to their source makes any hostility toward them unthinkable. Their mental ability to read and control our thoughts enables the twelve residents on our planet to move freely to anywhere at any time without fear of discovery, and opens to them any plot, scheme, or treachery. They cannot be fooled or deceived by any person on this planet. If they pose a threat to us, we would certainly have been enslaved or finished off long ago.

If their intention is to harm us, why would they delay plans for world domination until we have developed thermonuclear weapons and biological warfare? They could easily have eliminated a far smaller number of us when we were armed with nothing more potent than spears and stones. I believe their higher morality does not allow them to rub us out or manipulate our behavior in harmful ways. We are already more than able to do that for ourselves with no help from them. If their intent is to eliminate humanity, I have no doubt the easiest course would be to step back and allow us to destroy ourselves. Yet they continue to return, year after year, century after century, and work very hard while they are here.

We never saw them in the winter months when insects and plant life are dormant. Over the years since we first met them, people have been spraying great quantities of poison, including DDT, across the countryside to control insects. Since those times, we have realized what a terrible mistake we made with DDT and have changed our ways. The same is true with radioactive materials like the waste from mining and processing uranium, and the fallout from nuclear weapons and power plant disasters like Three Mile Island in the U.S. and Chernobyl in the Ukraine. We know now what terrible, long-term dangers such events present to ourselves as well as the planet. I think part of their work here was related to study of how we were poisoning the environment in those times. I think they were analyzing the grasshoppers, which eat a large amount of foliage, for chemical poisons in our environment. The reason they always seemed to be around in the afternoons through into the evenings is because that's when the bugs come out. We certainly had plenty of bugs in those years, if not much else.

My family often experienced the dark side of human nature. Now that I think back, Mike and I probably spent our time by ourselves out in the hills because we didn't get along with the kids in town. My father's people came to the United States from Germany when he was only seven years old. His father was a blacksmith. My mother's people came from Bohemia when she was three, and they were sheep ranchers. We spoke German at home more than English and were called foreigners and a lot of worse things than that. In the time when Hitler was coming to power in Germany, we came in for a lot of taunting and discrimination, but Dad was a hard worker and earned people's respect. He was badly hurt financially by the Depression and lost a large amount of money in a packing house business that failed between 1929 and 1930. I remember that he also lost thirty thousand dollars when the Flasher Bank failed. That was a lot more money back then than it is now. How many of us could stand up to that kind of loss today? I will always remember my father when he grabbed the neck-yoke from a wagon and used it to threaten two bankers who came to our place one day. Our family had to hold together when Mom died. I know the effort to save her cost Dad a large sum of money that he didn't have, to pay for medical bills.

We did not experience discrimination, suspicion, greed, and hatred when we were with these people from the stars. That is the most important thing I can tell you about them. They are kind and understanding and love us in spite of our dangerous behavior. I know they will do everything they can to help us learn from our mistakes and improve our lives as we grow into more mature and responsible behavior. Because of their concern for us, they will not give us dangerous tools or abilities we are not mature enough to handle and use, to lessen their burden of maintaining the planet. Think what it must cost them in terms of their own economy to build and send these ships to our world. Think what an individual sacrifice these men make by leaving behind the benefits and conveniences of their world to spend years of their lives analyzing grasshoppers on our world. These great men willingly took the time to speak to two grubby little farm kids in North Dakota and changed our lives forever.